The Windows® 95 Bug Collection

fixes and work-arounds for nearly 1,000 pesky problems when running Windows® 95

by Bruce Brown

and the editors of BugNet™
with Bruce Kratofil, Nigel R.M. Smith and Lane Morgan

Illustrations by Ed Solem

Addison-Wesley Publishing Company
Reading, Massachusetts · Menlo Park, California
New York · Don Mills, Ontario · Wokingham, England
Amsterdam · Bonn · Sydney · Singapore · Tokyo
Madrid · San Juan · Paris · Seoul · Milan
Mexico City · Taipei

Many of the designations used by manufacturers and sellers to distinguish their products are claimed as trademarks. Where those designations appear in this book, and Addison-Wesley was aware of a trademark claim, the designations have been printed in initial capital letters or all capital letters.

The author and publisher have taken care in preparation of this book, but make no expressed or implied warranty of any kind and assume no responsibility for errors or omissions. No liability is assumed for incidental or consequential damages in connection with or arising out of the use of the information or programs contained herein.

Library of Congress Cataloging-in-Publication Data

Brown, Bruce R.
The Windows 95 bug collection : fixes and work-arounds of pesky problems when running Windows 95 / by Bruce Brown ; and the editors of BugNet with Bruce Kratofil and Nigel R. M. Smith.
p. cm.
Includes index.
ISBN 0-201-48995-3
1. Microsoft Windows 95. 2. Operating Systems (Computers) I. Kratofil, Bruce. II. Smith, Nigel R. M. III. Title.
QA76.76.063B744 1996
005.4 ' 469--dc20
95-38809
CIP

Copyright © 1996 by Bruce Brown

All rights reserved. No part of this publication may be reproduced, stored in a retrieval system, or transmitted, in any form or by any means, electronic, mechanical, photocopying, recording, or otherwise, without the prior written permission of the publisher. Printed in the United States of America. Published simultaneously in Canada.

Sponsoring Editor: Kathleen Tibbetts
Cover design: Ann Gallager

1 2 3 4 5 6 7 8 9 -DOH- 0099989796
First printing, December 1995

Addison-Wesley books are available for bulk purchases by corporations, institutions, and other organizations. For more information please contact the Corporate, Government, and Special Sales Department at (800) 238-9682.

Find us on the World-Wide Web at:
http://www.aw.com/devpress/

Contents

Preface

You hold in your hands the most complete listing of Windows 95 bugs and fixes available anywhere, in any form.

The editors of BugNet have assembled this often requested "master list" to make your Windows 95 experience pleasant and trouble-free. Our primary aim is to provide solutions for as many Windows 95 problems as possible.

And where no fixes or work-arounds are available, we want to warn you so you can steer clear of the potholes. It's amazing how many people blunder into the same software problems day after day, simply because they don't know the problems exist.

Please understand, though, that bug/fix lists are by their nature very *dynamic*. Everything is a moving target. The manufacturers are constantly fixing bugs with one hand while they create them with the other.

You can't simply assume that a product doesn't work because it is listed here. By the time you read this, it may have been fixed. We recommend checking with the manufacturers in question for the current status of issues that may affect you.

It's also important to understand that all the bugs discussed here have met rigorous standards. All are reproducible, and have been confirmed by the manufacturer, a sysop or wizop on a forum that deals with the product, or two independent users.

We have thrown away 100 bug reports for every one included here. This is the "good stuff," collected from all across the PC universe, and put at your disposal.

May you go with foreknowledge.

– Bruce Brown
BugNet

Chapter 1
-- Installing Windows 95

Are you the kind of person who always gets a window seat?

Are you the sort of person who never gets a traffic ticket? Who never misses ferries? Who always gets a window seat?

Then read no further. This is for people who don't lead charmed lives -- and plan to install Windows 95 before too long.

Microsoft describes Windows 95 as "the most tested product in the history of the [software] industry," and it's true. In many respects, Windows 95 is much more stable and hassle-free than its predecessor, Windows 3.1.

A preliminary survey by BugNet of Windows 95 beta problems indicates that Microsoft fixed hundreds of major incompatibilities before the final release. In fact, with the exception of a few howlers (like the new WordScan 4 from Caere, which won't run on Windows 95, even though the previous WordScan 3 will), the backward compatibility provided by Windows 95 is impressive.

Most people who migrate to Windows 95 will experience little or no difficulty, but then most people who bought General Motors C and K style pickups haven't had any trouble either. Only a few have exploded into flames when hit from the side.

With a little planning, you can make your route into Windows 95 as safe and boring as possible. For instance, if the idea of reinstalling all your current Windows applications doesn't sound alluring, you should know that you won't have to if you install Windows 95 into the same directory as your current version of Windows.

Be aware, however, that if you DO install Windows 95 into the same directory where you currently have Windows (typically, C:\WINDOWS), you will not be able to dual-boot between Windows 95 and Windows 3.1, Windows for Workgroups 3.1, or Windows NT.

You will also lose your Windows 3.x applets, notably Windows Write and Paintbrush. Oddly enough, the Windows 95 versions of these mini-programs are inferior to their Windows 3.x predecessors.

It is possible, as Brian Livingston has shown in <u>InfoWorld</u>, to trick the Windows 95 installation procedure, and preserve your old Windows 3.x applets when you install Windows 95 over an existing Windows setup, but this is not for the uninitiated.

Besides, you can only take planning so far. You never know when the unexpected is going to happen, except it happens every day. Let's say you're in the middle of installing Windows 95 when a semi-truck full of Kevin Costner dolls crashes into the local power substation, causing a mediagenic power outage.

Bug/Fix Success Rates for Installation

The raw success rate for Windows 95 on Installation related issues is a very respectible 95 percent. There have been installation problems, but there are fixes for almost all of them.

Biggest Installation Problem

It appears the the people who are having the least problems installing Windows 95 are those who haven't had to install much, namely people who are buying new machines with Windows 95 and a bunch of 32-bit software pre-loaded.

Biggest Surprise

Windows 95 won't install on some genuine Intel 386s.

What do you do? Fear not. Windows 95 has this sort of situation well in hand. If Setup fails to complete due to a system freeze up, power interruption or other problem, turn off the machine, turn it back on, and restart Setup. DO NOT delete any files from the disk before restarting setup.

When you restart Setup, choose Smart Recovery and continue the setup procedure. If you encounter additional crashes after starting Smart Recovery, repeat the procedure a couple of times. Even if it takes more than one try, you should be able to get through it. Same goes for when your kid kicks out the power cord, or any other unplanned interruption of the installation process.

One of the biggest improvements in Windows 95 is the fact that its error messages frequently offer useful advice that can help you troubleshoot and correct problems (what a concept!). There is still plenty of cryptic gibberish, but with Windows 95 you can't assume (as was generally the case in previous versions of Windows) that every error message will be utterly useless.

Don't get too cocky, though. Along with the improvements, Windows 95 reduxes a cheap horror flick, *The Son of Copy Protection*. The DMF format used by Microsoft to distribute Windows 95 on disk is not compatible with normal high density floppies, and therefore you can not make backups of your system disks. Trash those suckers and you'll have to go on your hands and knees to Redmond for replacements.

If you get Windows 95 on CD-ROM instead of floppy disks, you have a little more latitude. You can use the TRANSFER.BAT tool on the Windows 95 Preview Program CD-ROM to create disk images of your CD system disk to your harddrive.

And speaking of backups, you have backed up everything that matters to you, haven't you? Any time you upgrade an operating system, it is a good idea to back up critical business or personal data.

Before you install Windows 95, Microsoft also recommends disabling all terminate-and-stay-resident (TSR) programs, such as anti-virus utilities, screen savers, disk scan utilities, undelete utilities, and the like.

Also, you should replace third-party memory managers such as QEMM and 386MAX with the plain vanilla

Microsoft equivalent HIMEM.SYS and EMM386.EXE before running Windows 95 Setup.

So now you're ready for the big plunge. Everything will probably be as smooth as you-know-what, but if you run into trouble, here are some work-arounds and fixes for some things that can cause difficulty installing Windows 95.

Enjoy!

Windows 95 Installation Bug & Fix List

The famous Generic Install Error and much more...

✔ If you are having problems installing applications from the floppy drive on your **Compaq** because the machine appears to hang with the drive light on, a temporary workround is to rename the file HSFLOP.PDR (in the WINDOWS\SYSTEM\IOSUBSYS folder) to HSFLOP.BAK and reboot the system. This will disable high speed data transfer under Windows 95.

✔ When you are running Windows 95 Setup on a **Dell** computer with a PCI bus, the detection process may stop at 80 percent complete. When this occurs, you see the error message

```
Divide By Zero
```

If you restart the computer and use Safe Recovery to finish Setup, more than one logical drive letter may be assigned to a single SCSI drive in the computer if they have two

---

Bug & Fix List Legend: The symbol 🐞 denotes bugs, incompatibilities and other difficulties. The symbol ✔ denotes problems which have either been fixed, or resolved with some sort of acceptable work-around. Products are listed in alphabetical order.

SCSI controllers. For example, when you try to access drive E you see the contents of drive C instead. The work-around is to disable the built-in SCSI controller and use the new controller for all the SCSI devices. Otherwise, you can use the second SCSI controller only for external devices. Use the built-in SCSI controller only for internal devices.

✔ If you receive the following message at the start of the Windows 95 Setup program

```
Setup Error G1. Windows Setup cannot
install from MS-DOS with EMM386.EXE or
similar utilities loaded on this ma-
chine. You will need to remove
EMM386.EXE from your CONFIG.SYS file and
restart your machine before running
Setup. After Windows has been installed,
you can safely add EMM386.EXE back to
your CONFIG.SYS.
```

Microsoft says this is caused by BIOS chips used in some **Gateway 2000** computers. The work-around, as the error message says (!), is to remove EMM386.EXE (or the similar memory manager) before you run Setup. Otherwise you need to upgrade your BIOS.

✔ If you have **DR-DOS** commands in your AUTOEXEC.BAT or CONFIG.SYS files when you attempt to install Windows 95, you will receive the error:

```
Warning SU-0019
```

Among the commands that can cause this error are: GOSUB, HILOAD, RETURN, SWITCH, CHAIN, HIBUFFERS, HIDEVICE, HIDOS, HIINSTALL, HISTORY, RETURN, SWITCH, TIMEOUT, BASEDEV, DEVINFO, DISKCACHE, IFS, IOPL, LIBPATH, MAXWAIT, MEMMAN,

PRINTMONBUFSIZE, DPRIORITY_DISK_IO, PROTECTONLY, PROTSHELL, SWAPPATH, THREADS
The work-around: you must remove these before you can install Windows 95.

✔ If during the first reboot in Windows 95 Setup, you receive the error message:

```
Invalid system disk
Replace the disk, and then press any key
```

you can be suffering from one of several maladies: (1) your system may infected with a boot-sector virus such as the AntiCMOS.A virus, (2) your system may be running virus-protection software, (3) your system may be using hard disk management software (such as **Disk Manager**, **EZ-Drive**, or **DrivePro**). If so, run your old anti-virus software, and then turn off virus protection and disk management software. If you have virus protection in your BIOS, rather than software (the Award BIOS is one that has the anti-virus feature, also known as Boot Sector Protection), contact the manufacturer for more information.

✔ Here's a little blow to the kneecap of **IBM** -- and you too if you own a Micro Channel computer. After installing Windows 95 on an IBM 9353 computer with a standard IDE hard disk and controller, you may get the following error:

```
Windows has detected that your computer
is not configured for its fastest pos-
sible performance. Would you like to see
more information about this problem?
```

followed by

```
Compatibility mode paging reduces over-
all system performance. Drive C: using
MS-DOS compatibility mode.
```

The problem is that Windows 95 does not detect standard IDE hard disks on MCA computers. The work-around: manually add the ESDI/IDE driver to get 32-bit protected-mode functionality:

1. Click the Start button, point to Settings, and then click Control Panel.
2. Double-click the Add New Hardware icon, and then click Next.
3. Click No, and then click Next.
4. Click Hard Disk Controllers, and then click Next.
5. In the Models box, click Standard IDE/ESDI Controller, and then click Next.
6. Accept the default resource settings for the device. Click Next.

(NOTE: this will only work if the computer is configured for standard resources. If it isn't, these settings may not work correctly and will have to be set manually.

7. click Finish, then restart the computer when you are prompted to do so.

¥ You may find you find you can't install Windows 95 on an **Intel 80386** computer, and get the following error:

```
Setup error B1: Setup has detected an
80386 processor that is not compatible
with this version of Windows. Before you
can run this version of Windows, you
need to upgrade your processor. Contact
your computer manufacturer for more
information.
```

The problem is that Intel 386 microprocessors dated before April 1987 are known as B1 stepping chips. These chips are known to introduce random math errors when performing 32-bit operations, thus making them incompatible with Windows 95. You need a new machine to run Windows 95.

✔ If you install **Microsoft Plus!** for Windows 95 on a computer using a 16-color video driver, you may receive the following message:

```
Because your display is currently set to
256 colors, Setup will install only the
256-color desktop themes. If your dis-
play can be reconfigured for more col-
ors, you might also want to install the
high-color themes. Install high-color
themes too?
```

The problem is that there is a bug in Microsoft Plus! for Windows 95 which causes it to only detect that you are not using a High Color device, without distinguishing between 16- and 256-color displays. The work-around: do not install the Visual Enhancements components on a computer with a 16-color palette. "The desktop themes are designed for use on a computer using 256 or more colors," according to Microsoft.

✔ When you run Windows 95 Setup on a system that has the **OS/2** Boot Manager partition active, you will receive an error message such as:

```
Setup has detected a boot manager parti-
tion on your system.
```

Continuing Setup will disable Boot Manager. If you continue, Windows 95 Setup will indeed disable the Boot Manager. To reactivate the OS/2 Boot Manager, boot the system from the OS/2 boot disk and then run the Fdisk utility.

✔**Windows 95** may freeze during Setup or when it attempts to load on an Acma Pentium 120, or any machine that uses Award Modular BIOS v4.50G, copyright 1994-1995, or a 586 PCI Green BIOS 52xver, according to Microsoft. You are then asked whether you want to overwrite the boot sector. Choosing Yes may allow you to complete the Setup procedure, but Windows 95 hangs when it attempts to load. Then, after you restart the computer, you may get the following:

```
Windows Setup was unable to update your
system files.
```

This may be caused by virus detection that is built-in to your machine, or by virus detection software running on your system. You must disable these virus protection features to install Windows 95.

✔ If you try to install **Windows 95** on a computer that used to have Windows NT installed on it, Setup may report that Windows NT is still installed, even though it is not. The work-around: quit Setup, delete the WINVER.EXE file from the WINDOWS\SYSTEM32 folder, and then run Setup again.

✔ If your computer freezes on the "**Windows 95** is now setting up your hardware and any Plug and Play devices you may have" screen the first time you reboot after installing Windows 95, the problem is probably a damaged .INF file. The work-around: remove all the files in the hidden Windows\INF folder:

1. At an MS-DOS prompt, type the following line and then press ENTER:

```
attrib -h c:\windows\inf
```

2. Type the following line, then press ENTER:

```
cd c:\windows\inf
```

3. Type the following line, then press ENTER:

```
ren *.inf *.old
```

✔ If during the installation of **Windows 95**, you receive the following error message:

```
Setup Detection Warning
Warning SU-0014
```

Then Setup has found a hardware device on your computer that is not responding. Click Continue to try this device again. If problems persist, click Exit Setup, quit all programs, remove floppy disks from their drives, and turn your computer off. Then, turn your computer on and run Setup again (choose Safe Recovery when prompted).

This error message can be caused if your network, CD-ROM, or floppy drive has stopped responding for some \reason. The work-around: follow the error message instructions.

✔ If your hard disk does not have at least 3 megs. of free space after installing **Windows 95**, or if your hard disk contains bad sectors, you may get the following error

```
Windows could not combine VxDs into a
monolithic file before starting.
Windows may not start or run properly.
```

when your computer restarts after Setup. The work-around: delete some files from your harddrive, and use a utility like SCANDISK to fix bad clusters.

✔ When **Windows 95** is detecting the hardware in your computer during installation, you may get an error like:

```
SDMErr(80000003): Registry access
failed.
```

if your registry has become corrupted. The work-around:

1. Restart your computer. When you see the "Starting Windows 95" message, press the F8 key, and then choose Safe Mode Command Prompt Only from the Startup menu.
2. Type the following at the MS-DOS prompt, and then press ENTER:

```
regedit /e reg.txt
```

(IMPORTANT: Ignore any message about missing data.)
3. Type the following, and then press ENTER:

```
regedit /c reg.txt
```

4. Restart the computer normally, and go back and rerun the operation that caused the error message in the first place.

✔ Microsoft has acknowledged "isolated reports" that a virus was corrupting the second **Windows 95** installation disk. According to Microsoft, the second of 13 diskettes used to install Windows 95 can be corrupted by certain unspecified viruses already present on a user's PC (the CD-ROM version of Windows 95 is unaffected). Microsoft suggests two preventive measures to deal with the disk 2 problem. One is to run an antivirus program on the PC prior to upgrading to Windows 95 to eliminate any viruses. The second is to write-protect the installation diskettes by flipping up the tab in the diskettes' upper-lefthand corner. That will prevent a diskette from being written to, but it won't do anything about viruses already present on the PC.

✔ When you are installing **Windows 95**, you may receive the following error

```
Generic install error Invalid GenInstall
INF file. -[Exiting with error code =
402(0x192).]
```

When you choose OK, the Setup program terminates. This error occurs if the existing WIN.INI file contains a LOAD entry that does not have an equal sign (=).To fix the problem, edit your WIN.INI file and either remove the LOAD entry or add an equal sign to the entry (so that it reads "LOAD=") and then run the Windows 95 Setup program again.

✔ If setup hangs while making a startup disk, you can either remove device=symevnt.386 in the [386enh] section of your SYSTEM.INI and rerun Setup, or run Setup without making a startup disk. After Setup completes, you can make one through Add/Remove Programs in the **Windows 95** Control Panel.

✔ If you receive a message that The path <xxx> is invalid When you try to set up **Windows 95**, the problem is that you are trying to install Windows 95 on a drive that has zero (0) bytes available. You need to free some disk space, or install to another drive.

✔ If you receive a general protection fault in USER.EXE and Setup error SU0410 when installing **Windows 95**, Microsoft recommends that you disable SMARTDrive in the AUTOEXEC.BAT file and run Setup with the /IC switch. The /IC switch causes Windows 95 Setup to not load its own version of SMARTDrive.

✔ When you run **Windows 95** Setup on an Acer portable computer, Setup may not finish successfully. The reason is that the default advanced power management (APM) settings on Acer portable computers can cause interruptions in the Setup process. To install Windows 95, you must first disable the APM features in CMOS memory. For information about how to modify CMOS settings, please consult the computer's documentation.

✔ To upgrade from **Windows 3.0** to **Windows 95**, you must run Setup from DOS and choose to install Windows 95 in the same directory as Windows 3.0 was installed.

✔ If **Windows 95** Setup hangs during the "routine check on your system" while it's running ScanDisk, try to find out why ScanDisk is hanging by running a virus check and running ScanDisk at the MS-DOS level. Microsoft advises trying both these options before using the switch Setup /IS to disable ScanDisk.

✔ If it seems that **Windows 95** Setup is hanging, but there is still hard drive activity, Microsoft advises that you try to be patient and wait it out.

✔ If **Windows 95** Setup hangs during reboot, look for lines in SYSTEM.INI pointing to an old swapfile and comment them out.

✔ **Windows 95** may freeze during Setup or when it attempts to load. You are then asked whether you want to overwrite the boot sector. Choosing Yes may allow you to complete the Setup procedure, but Windows 95 hangs when it attempts to load. Then, after you restart the computer, you get the following:

```
Windows Setup was unable to update your
system files.
```

This may be caused by virus detection that is built-in to your machine, or by virus detection software running on your system. You must disable these virus protection features to install Windows 95.

✔ If you try to install programs or device drivers that require that an AUTOEXEC.BAT or CONFIG.SYS file be present on your hard disk, the installation may fail in **Windows 95**. These files are not required in Windows 95, and they may not be present on your system. The work-around: create generic AUTOEXEC.BAT and CONFIG.SYS files and place them in the root directory of your boot drive.

✔ If you try to install **Windows 95** and encounter the error:

```
Setup checked the hard disk(s) on your
computer and found that there may be a
problem.
```

And then you get the error again after you run

```
SCANDISK.EXE /ALL
```

try running good old

```
CHKDISK /F
```

and then reinstall Windows 95.

Chapter 2 -- Windows 95 Utilities

Return with us now to those thrilling days of yesteryear!

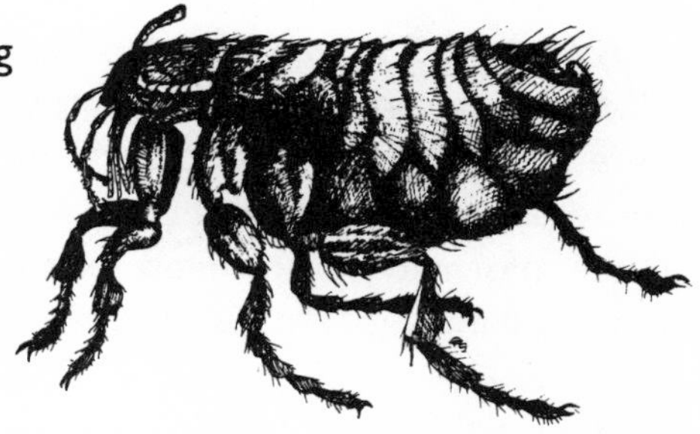

When reading about the pioneer days in the Old West, you may have wondered what it would be like to load all your belongings onto a covered wagon and head off across the frontier to start a new life.

Well, the West is settled now, but you can get a little of that pioneer feeling by packing up all your software onto the ol' hard drive, and bravely heading for a new operating system. As you do, remember the old saying: You can tell the pioneers — they're the ones with the arrows in their backs.

On the Windows 95 frontier, the arrows are flying thick and heavy in the Utilities section, and with good reason.

Windows 3.1 and its kin were written to run on top of Microsoft DOS, which was a fully functioning operating system that needed to boot up completely before you could run Windows.

However, Windows 95 boots up directly, even though it does make use of parts of DOS. There are enough changes to DOS that many people are referring to it as DOS 7, even though it is not an official, separate product upgrade.

These changes are an obstacle to many traditional utility programs that are written to work directly with prior versions of DOS and Windows. They expect things to be a certain way, and Windows 95 often confounds them. So it pays to be very careful in dealing with utilities such as anti-virus software, disk stackers, memory managers, and back-up programs. Utilities that are meant to be run from a DOS command line may be particularly suspect.

Windows 95's new long file name feature causes grief in a lot of these programs. When most of the 16-bit utilities were written, there was no such thing as long file names. These programs look to the File Allocation Table (FAT) for all the information they need. Yet the information about the long file names is kept elsewhere (in the Virtual File Allocation Table).

This makes old Windows 3.1 data recovery tools, back-up programs, disk stackers, etc. very vulnerable to corruption or loss. Desktop shell programs that replace Program Manager are typically be rendered useless also.

Another area of major concern is anti-virus software. Since 16-bit applications are supposed to work under Windows 95, it is not surprising that 16-bit viruses will, too. (Of course, Microsoft won't be bragging about backward-compatibility here.) But 16-bit anti-virus software that is designed to run in the background will have trouble running under Windows 95 — in fact you must disable all

Bug/Fix Success Rates for Utilities

The raw bug/fix success rate for Windows utilities running under Windows 95 is horrible, just 16 percent. Until new 32-bit Windows 95-compatible utilities appear, look lively!

Biggest Utility Problem

Windows 95's new long file name feature probably causes more trouble than anything else for legacy Windows utilities.

Biggest Surprise (Not)

Microsoft and Quarterdeck are arguing over whether it is advisable to use QEMM with Windows 95 (guess who says what).

existing anti-virus software AND hardware in order to install Windows 95.

The problem is that Windows 95 does not come with anti-virus software of its own, and as of this writing there is precious little new 32-bit anti-virus software on the market, which opens up a window of opportunity for these system-wreckers. It is one of these viruses, for instance, that is responsible for the "disk 2" problem that has foiled some Windows 95 installations. (For this reason, it is a good idea to run an anti-virus check on your system under

Windows 3.1 before letting down your shield and installing Windows 95.)

Fact is, despite all of Windows 95's allure and advancements, you will still need a handful of utilities to perform many of the same tasks you used them for under Windows 3.1 or DOS, but you probably won't be able to use your old standbys.

This is even true for extended memory managers. Even though Windows 95's memory management is vastly superior to that of Windows 3.1, you may still need a third party memory manager like Netroom or QEMM, especially if you plan to use demanding "legacy" DOS applications like games.

Unfortunately, many people who've had problems running QEMM with Windows 95 say that Microsoft Technical Support is advising people that QEMM is incompatible with Windows 95 and should be removed. Technical Support for Quarterdeck, the makers of QEMM, responds that their product is in fact compatible, but it does need some tweaking.

As this is being written, the various utility companies are rushing development on the upgrades needed to make their programs Windows 95-compatible. So consult the following list closely, and if you have any doubts, contact the company for more information.

Then maybe you won't become the computer equivalent of the Donner Party.

Windows 95 Utilities Bug & Fix List

After Dark, Norton Utilities, Carbon Copy, QEMM, Laplink, Stacker and much more...

¥ Your computer may freeze if you have more than 16 megs, of RAM and **386MAX** istalled. The work-around: remove 386Max and use the Microsoft XMS memory manager (HIMEM.SYS) instead by removing any reference to 386MAX in your CONFIG.SYS and then adding:

```
device=c:\windows\himem.sys
```

You should then save your CONFIG.SYS and restart your computer.

¥ Users of **386MAX 6.01d and 7.0** from Qualitas may experience configuration problems in Windows 95. Check the release notes for information, and contact the manufacturer if necessary.

Bug & Fix List Legend: The symbol ¥ denotes bugs, incompatibilities and other difficulties. The symbol ✔ denotes problems which have either been fixed, or resolved with some sort of acceptable work-around. Products are listed in alphabetical order.

✔ **4DOS 4.0 and 4.01** by JP Software were designed for an earlier version of MS-DOS. You will need to upgrade to at least version 5.5. See also comments for 4DOS 5.5.

✔ The problem with **4DOS 5.5** by JP Software is that it generally replaces COMMAND.COM. Then the WIN command isn't run automatically as it is in Windows 95. The workaround: put a WIN command in AUTOEXEC.BAT.

¥ Berkeley Systems **After Dark 1.0 for DOS** will not run correctly under Windows 95. It will not activate after the set amount of time or by using the hotkey. Also once it is installed, all other file operations will slow down. The Windows version of this program runs fine; contact the manufacturer.

¥ Running Berkeley Systems **After Dark 2.0** with Windows 95, you may see some weirdness. To wit: when you install the After Dark screen saver, an After Dark button may be created on the taskbar; however, clicking this button with the left mouse button does not open the After Dark control panel. Also, a blank button may appear on the taskbar when the After Dark screen saver is active. Or a button labeled "Password" appears on the taskbar when the Password dialog box appears. According to Berkeley Systems Technical Support, After Dark version 2.0 for Windows and its add-on components based on the After Dark 2.0 engine are not fully compatible with Windows 95. The work-around: if you click the After Dark button using the right (secondary mouse button, the Control menu appears. The After Dark control panel is one of the selections. You can also click the After Dark icon on the desktop, rather than the button on the taskbar, to open the After Dark control panel.

¥ In Berkeley Systems **After Dark 3.0 for Windows**, you may get errors when running Bad Dog if Windows 95 is an upgrade from **Windows 3.x**.

¥ Microcom's **Carbon Copy 2.5** and below for Windows won't run on Windows 95, although they will perform some functions under MS-DOS Mode. Windows 95 Setup removes the DOSHOST.EXE TSR if it is loaded in either AUTOEXEC.BAT or CONFIG.SYS; otherwise, the system will stall. Windows 95 Help automatically provides information.

✔ Like all MS-DOS-based remote control programs **Carbon Copy 6.1 for DOS** from Microcom requires MS-DOS Mode. CCHELP.EXE (the host) is set to run automatically in MS-DOS Mode; CC.EXE (the guest) should also be run in MS-DOS but will not do so automatically.

✔ **Central Point Anti-Virus for Windows 1.0, 2.0, and 2.1** were designed to work with Windows 3.1, so some of their features may not work correctly under Windows 95. Windows 95 Help automatically provides a warning. Contact the manufacturer for an updated version

✔ Because Windows 95 Setup requires that VSAFE.COM be removed before upgrading from Windows 3.1, some features of **Central Point Anti-Virus for DOS 1.4 and 2.1** do not work correctly under Windows 95. Contact the manufacturer for an updated version.

✔ If **Windows 95** freezes at the Windows 95 logo screen the first time you start it after upgrading, the problem may be that you have **Microsoft Anti-Virus, Norton Anti-Virus** or **Central Point Anti-Virus** loading automatically from your AUTOEXEC.BAT file. The work-around: pressing the ESC key closes the Windows 95 logo screen and allows you to access the anti-virus application. Choose the option that allows the application to update any affected files. This prevents the pause from occurring when you start Windows 95 in the future.

¥ Quarterdeck **CleanSweep** is compatible with Windows 95. However, it will ignore long file names and will deal only with the 8.3 version of the name.

¥ Norton-Lambert **Close-Up Customer/Terminal 4.0** for DOS is not supported under Windows 95. Contact the manufacturer to get a version that works.

¥ Norton-Lambert's **Close-Up 6.0** in the MS-DOS-based version does not work correctly as the host under Windows 95. Transmission stops when the task is switched to background, and reception stops shortly thereafter. Contact manufacturer for a Windows 95 version.

¥ **Colorado Backup 2.02, 2.5, 2.54, and 4.03** were designed to work with the MS-DOS file system and they do not recognize the long file names used by Windows 95. Contact the manufacturer for an update.

¥ **Conner Backup Exec 2.1** was designed to work with the MS-DOS file system and does not recognize Windows 95 long filenames. Contact the manufacturer for an updated version.

¥ Quarterdeck **DataSafe** is incompatible with Windows 95.

¥ **Data Safe 2.0** by Landmark Research's control panel cannot correctly list the active tasks in Windows 95, and the system becomes unstable after using Data Safe for a while, reporting errors for clicking on title bars. Remove Data Safe before installing Windows 95, or install a later version.

✔ Quarterdeck **DESQview** is compatible with MS-DOS 7. This is the DOS version that ships with Windows 95. You can run it in a DOS window, but without the features that require QEMM386. To use these features, you have to exit Windows 95 via the "Boot to DOS" method.

✔ **DESQview/X** is compatible with **MS-DOS 7**. However, it will not run in a Windows 95 DOS window. You will have to exit Windows 95 via the "Boot to DOS" method.

✔ If Fifth Generation Systems **Direct Access 5.1** gets about 60 percent through installation under Windows 95 and then stalls, install from MS-DOS mode instead.

¥ In AddStor **Double Tools 1.0, 1.36**, the DBLSPACE.BIN from DoubleTools is incompatible with Windows 95. Installing this utility will cause loss of any DriveSpace compressed drives until the Microsoft DBLSPACE.BIN is copied back to the host drive to replace the Double Tools version. There is no update version of this program available at press time. Check Windows 95 Help for more information.

✔ **Grabit Pro 4.2 for Windows NT** from Software Excellence By Design will create the program icon incorrectly when installed using the Add/Remove Program wizard, but will be correct if Windows Explorer is used.

¥ **Grabit Pro 4.2 for Windows NT** from Software Excellence By Design cannot change the default printer under Windows 95.

¥ **I/RAS B 5.1 for Windows NT** by Integraph cannot run under Windows 95. It goes astray during setup when it looks for Windows NT Administrative Privileges to install. Integraph may make an updated setup program available.

¥ Moon Valley **Icon Do-It 1.0 for Windows** may not work correctly. When Do It On Your Desktop is started, the program may stop running.

¥ In Moon Valley's **Icon Hear It Too! 1.0a**, Fun With Sounds does not work. You cannot animate icons or cursors. The program's window also covers the Windows 95 minimize/maximize buttons with its button.

✔ Quarterdeck claims its **Internet Suite** is fully compatible running as a 16-bit application under Windows 95, but acknowledges that there are a few small problems with the display in the Quarterdeck Message Center.

✔ Traveling Software **LapLink (V)**, unlike some of its siblings, will run in Windows 95 if you delete the LL.PIF file. Windows 95 provides information automatically.

✔ **LapLink Pro (V) 4.0a** by Traveling Software requires MS-DOS Mode.

¥ **Lightning Cache 1.2 for Windows** by Lucid is not supported by Windows 95.

¥ Quarterdeck's **MagnaRAM** is incompatible with Windows 95.

¥ **Manifest 3.0** (and all later versions) is a combined DOS and Windows program. If you run it in a DOS window under Windows 95, the Windows version of Manifest will execute, and TECHSUP.BAT will not work properly. As a workaround, when you run Manifest, select the option "All of Manifest to be printed to a file."

¥ Artisoft's **MORE 3.01 for Windows** cannot run correctly under Windows 95 because the video drivers are incompatible.

✔ According to Helix, the **Netroom** Cloaked Disk Cache may interfere with installation of Windows 95 from floppy disk. The work-around: disable the Netroom cache during installation by REMarking out the CACHECLK line in your AUTOEXEC.BAT prior to installing Windows 95.

✔ Due to a bug in the BIOS.VXD Windows 95 device driver, some systems with plug and play BIOSs may encounter a lockup loading or installing Windows 95 if **Netroom**'s System BIOS Cloaking is enabled. The work-around: obtain a patch is available to the Netroom RMLODHI.VXD from Helix.

✔ On some systems Windows 95 will enter "Compatibility Mode" when **Netroom**'s System BIOS Cloaking is enabled. To prevent this, Helix advises adding "SYSCLOAK.EXE" to the IOS.INI file in the Windows directory.

✔ According to Helix, you may safely ignore any Windows 95 warnings regarding RM386 when installing Windows 95 on a system with **Netroom 2**. Once Windows 95 is installed, run Customize as follows:

1. Restart Windows and when you see the "Starting Windows 95" message, press the SHIFT-F5 key combination. The shift F5 key combination is accomplished by holding down the SHIFT keys while the PC is rebooting then pressing the F5 key as soon as the "Starting Windows 95" message appears. This bypasses your startup files and gets you to a DOS prompt.

2. You will need to edit the file named MSDOS.SYS. This file is normally hidden and cannot be edited until its attribute is changed. To change the attributes for MSDOS.SYS type the following commands from the DOS prompt:

```
ATTRIB MSDOS.SYS -R -S -H
```

3. Then, from the DOS prompt type

```
EDIT MSDOS.SYS
```

Your screen should contain a line with the option

```
BootGUI=1
```

Replace the "1" with "0" (zero). This will tell Windows not to boot automatically into Windows whenever you start up your PC. Directly under the "BootGUI=1" line, add a line that contain the parameter

```
Logo=0
```

This turns off the display of the Windows 95 logo which interferes with the operation of Customize and VIDCLOAK. Now save and exit MSDOS.SYS.

4. Restart the PC and you'll see that Windows will no longer start up automatically (type "WIN" from the DOS prompt at any time to execute Windows). Change directory to Netroom and run Customize Normally.

5. To start Windows, type "WIN" at the MS-DOS prompt. If you wish, you may edit the MSDOS.SYS file and restore the

```
BootGUI=1
```

in order to load Windows automatically after processing your AUTOEXEC.BAT. If, after running Customize, you have a problem starting Windows, Helix advises that you download the RMLODHI.VXD Windows 95 patch found in Library section 13 in the CompuServe PCVENG forum, and on the Helix BBS at 718-392-4054.

¥ **NewWave 4.1**'s shell replacement may not be fully functional in Windows 95. Contact Hewlett Packard for a compatible version.

¥ If you install Microsoft **PowerPoint 4.0** while running **Norton Desktop for Windows 2.0** as the shell, you may receive the following error:

```
Unable to Start DDE communications with
Program Manager
Abort, Retry, Ignore
```

Microsoft says, "Microsoft does not support using any shell other than WindowsExplorer as the primary Windows 95 shell. If you want to use a third-party shell with Windows 95, Microsoft recommends adding it to the Startup folder."

¥ You may have problems with **Norton AntiVirus for Windows, Norton Utilities for Windows, Norton Navigator for Windows** if you install the final version of Windows 95 over the release 490 beta version. If you have 490 on your system, Symantec advises that you backup the entire machine, wipe everything clean, and then install Windows 95 and your other programs.

✔ The French Boot virus, which is detected by the **Norton Anti-Virus** 16 bit edition, is not listed in the 32-bit edition, Norton AntiVirus for Windows 95. The virus is still detected, however. Only now it is called the Jumper Virus.

✔ **Norton Utilities for Windows 95** will often report a higher degree of disk fragmentation than the Windows 95 Disk Defragmentor program. This is because the Norton program looks at and defragments hidden files while the Windows 95 program ignores them.

✔ If you receive the error message with **Norton AntiVirus for Windows 95**

```
NAVAPW32 caused an invalid page fault in
module KRNL386.EXE at 00001:00008016.
```

the problem may be in the Video Acceleration setting. Turning down the Video Acceleration under Properties of My Computer under the Performance tab/Video has worked for people with this problem.

✔ There is no replacement for the Data Sort utility in **Norton Utilities for Windows 95**. Since the Explorer windows are always sorted, this feature was left out of the new release.

¥ Some features of Symantec's **Norton Antivirus 2.0 and 2.1 for DOS and Windows** do not work correctly under Windows 95.

✔ Symantec's **Norton Backup 2.0 and 2.2 for DOS** require MS-DOS Mode.

¥ Some features of Symantec's **Norton Backup 2.0 and 3.0 for Windows** do not work correctly under Windows 95.

¥ With **Norton Desktop 2.0 for Windows** by Symantec, Windows Setup 95 removes the .NAV and .SYS anti-virus TSR from CONFIG.SYS and removes NAVPOPUP.EXE from WIN.INI load= entries. Some of this program's features do not work correctly under Windows 95.

¥ Some features of Symantec's **Norton Desktop 3.0 for Windows** do not work correctly under Windows 95. For example, program groups are not converted to the Windows 95 start menu.

¥ **Norton Speedrive** by Symantec does not work correctly under Windows 95. You can use the Disk Defragmenter provided with Windows 95.

¥ Some features of Symantec's **Norton Utilities 6.01, 7.0, and 8.0** and **Norton Utilities Administrator 1.0** do not work correctly under Windows 95.

¥ Some features of Symantec's **Norton Utilities 8.0 for Windows** do not work correctly under Windows 95.

¥ If you are running **Norton Antivirus** (NAVTSRW.EXE) from **Norton Desktop for Windows 3.0**, your system may freeze when you exit or shut down Windows 95. At this time, the only workaround is to remove or remark out the NAVTSRW.EXE line in your WIN.INI file.,

¥ OnTrack **DOS UTIL 3.14**'s scan function erroneously reports an increasing number of bad directories during runs because of Windows 95 long filenames.

¥ If you are running **pcAnywhere** under Windows 95, pcAnywhere will tend to monopolize the CPU, causing the rest of your software to run very slowly. According to Symantec Technical Support, "Just about any communications program that monitors the serial port but doesn't use the Windows 95 API for communications will have this problem." Feel better?

¥ Because of changes to the Windows operating system in Windows 95, Symantec's **pcANYWHERE 1.0 and 2.0 for Windows** generally does not work correctly under Windows 95. If you have to try, be sure to use a standard VGA driver.

✔ Symantec's **pcANYWHERE 4.5 and 5.0** require MS-DOS Mode when running. The PIF file provided with the program must be deleted or renamed in order for MS-DOS Mode to take effect.

¥ Multisoft's **PC-Kwik 2.1 and 3.1** do not work in Windows 95 because the Setup program removes them from AUTOEXEC.BAT. Windows 95 Help automatically provides information for obtaining an updated version.

✔ At the end of installing **Spatial Technology Personal ACIS**, you may receive the following error:

```
You still need to install the Win32S
subsystem before Personal ACIS will run.
```

even though Personal ACIS will run. Spatial Technology and Microsoft are aware of the problem.

¥ Atech Software's **Publishers PowerPak 2.1** does not work under Windows 95.

¥ Windows 95 Setup removes LaserTools **Print Cache** from AUTOEXEC.BAT, so it will not run.

¥ Funk Software's **Proxy 1.12 and 1.5**'s PHOST.EXE TSR must be loaded on the host, so it does not work for Windows 95 as the host. As a Master workstation, PROXY.EXE will correctly take over DOS and NetWare sessions, but not **Windows 3.x** sessions.

¥ **QAPlus 6.0** for Windows by DiagSoft may stall your system during Memory Check, IRQ Check, and Network Check.

¥ Quarterdeck's QEMM386.SYS is compatible with Windows 95, and can provide memory management for it and any programs loaded before it. However, the Windows 95 installation will automatically detect and disable QEMM's DOS-Up features, because it is incompatible with MS-DOS 7, the version of DOS that is included with Windows 95. The new version of DriveSpace included with Windows 95 is also incompatible with **QEMM 7.5** Stealth D*Space and **QEMM 7.0** Stealth DoubleSpace. Windows 95 will disable these drivers as well. For full details, refer to the file OPTWIN95.QKN, which is available as a technical note in library 3 of Quarterdeck's CompuServe forum.

✔The **QEMM** QuickBoot feature does not operate correctly in Windows 95. To prevent your computer from freezing, Microsoft advises that you disable QuickBoot. To do this, add the parameter

```
BOOTENABLE:N
```

to the QEMM386.SYS line in the CONFIG.SYS file. For example, after you add this parameter the line might look like:

```
DEVICE=<path>\QEMM386.SYS BOOTENABLE:N
```

¥ According to Microsoft, Users of Quarterdeck's **QEMM 386 6.01, 7.0 and 7.5** may experience configuration problems with Windows 95.

¥ **SideKick 1.5 for DOS** needs to be handled with care. Once Windows 95 is installed, using CTL+ALT to invoke Sidekick may cause SideKick to open inactive in full-screen mode unless MS-DOS Prompt is open. Once that happens you cannot subsequently restore Windows 95 screen and operation.

¥ When the mouse pointer is moved over any of the toolbar buttons, **SideKick 2.0 for Windows** redraws the title bar over the Windows 95 Close icon. The icon still works, though.

¥ **SideKick 2.0 for Windows** may display problems with To Do items.

¥ Vertisoft **SpaceManager 1.53** was not designed to work with MS-DOS 6.x DblSpace and does not perfom well under Windows 95, according to Microsoft.

¥ If you have **SoftRAM 1.03** installed on your computer, you may get the following error message on a blue screen:

```
Invalid VxD dynamic link call from
IOS[03] +00000B5D to device "Pagefile,"
service 7. Your Windows configuration is
```

```
invalid, run the windows Setup program
again to correct this problem.
```

This problem occurs because SoftRam 1.03 is incompatible with Windows 95. The work-around: disable SoftRAM.

¥ Syncronos Software acknowledges that **SoftRAM95 2.0** may cause data loss on Windows 95 systems when the user defragments a drive larger than 500 megs. (and these days, what drive isn't).

✔ **SoftTrack 2.0** from ON Technology will not work correctly under Windows 95 for Win32-based and MS-DOS-based programs, because it expects different attributes when files are opened. Win16 programs are metered correctly.

✔ If you are running **Stacker 4.1**, you can uncompress a stacked drive under Windows 95. There were reports on the Microsoft Windows 95 forum that this could not be done.

¥ If you want to run **Stacker Anywhere** on a PCMIA hard drive under Windows 95, you have to run the stacker program from DOS. To do this, reboot your computer and hold down the F8 key to step through the start-up procedure. Respond No when it asks if you want to start Windows. Then run Stacker Anywhere. Afterwards you can start Windows by typing WIN.

¥ No versions of **Stacker** prior to 4.1 can handle the long file names of Windows 95.

¥ STAC Electronics's **ReachOut/Pro Edition 4.04** does not work correctly under Windows 95. You'll see video display problems when using remote control.

¥ STAC Electronics **Multimedia Stacker 4.02** utilities can't deal with Windows 95 enhancements such as long filenames. Do not use this version of Stacker to compress, optimize, resize, uncompress, or change the expected compression ratio of drives on your system. Windows 95 Help automatically provides information for obtaining an updated version from the manufacturer.

¥ STAC Electronics **Stacker 3.0, 3.1 and 4.0** utilities are not aware of Windows 95 enhancements such as long filenames. Do not use this version of Stacker to compress, optimize, resize, uncompress, or change the expected compression ratio of drives on your system. Windows 95 Help automatically provides information for obtaining an updated version from the manufacturer.

✔ AddStor's **SuperStor 1.36** works under Windows 95, but there are a couple of pitfalls. See comments for AddStor SuperStor 2.0.

✔ Windows 95 will work correctly on AddStor's **SuperStor 2.0** drive, but performance may be slow. Also, you should not compress a drive using SuperStor once Windows 95 is installed because Windows ScanDisk and Defrag will not run on the compressed drive. Windows 95 Help automatically provides information.

¥ **Uninstaller 2.00.03** from Microhelp has display problems and terminates during certain operations because "uninstall" behavior is different under Windows 95 than under Windows 3.1.

¥ **Uninstall-It! 1.03** by Landmark Research International may produce garbage for Win32-based programs by erroneously extracting descriptions from EXE files, according to Microsoft.

¥ The IniExpert user interface does not display correctly under Windows 95 in Landmark Research International's **Uninstall-It! 1.03**.

¥ McAfee **Virus Scan 2.1** has difficulties with communications between the DOS TSR and Windows monitoring components.

¥ Quarterdeck **WebAuthor** will work correctly with Microsoft **Word for Windows 6** under Windows 95. However, WebAuthor is incompatible with Word for Office 95.

¥ When you run the **Windows 95** Disk Defragmenter tool on drive C, you may receive the following error message:

```
Error Defragmenting Drive C:\
Windows cannot defragment this drive now
because it has been locked by a disk
utility. Quit any utilities that may
have locked this drive, and then try
defragmenting the drive again. Microsoft
reports that "this error can occur under
the following conditions:
```

1) Drive C is attached to an IDE controller.
2) There is an **Adaptec AHA-1542C SCSI controller** with another hard disk attached to it in your computer.
3) The ID for the SCSI hard disk is set to 0 (zero).

To correct this problem, set the ID of the SCSI hard disk to anything except 0."

¥ The 16-bit version of Quarterdeck's **WinProbe** is incompatible with Windows 95

¥ Landmark Research's **WinProbe 2.1, 3.0.0 and 3.1** all have numerous problems and errors and do not perform satisfactorally under Windows 95, according to Microsoft.

¥ If **XTree 2.0 for Windows** gives you the message:

```
Not enough memory or resources to open
the dialog
```

during attempts to make network connections, you'll need an updated version.

¥ **XTree Gold 2.54** may have trouble with commands such as Graft, Prune, and Disk Formatting. You will need to delete the PIF before use in order to see information provided by Windows 95 Help for obtaining an update from the manufacturer.

¥ Symantec's **XTree Gold 4.0 for Windows** is not fully functional. Undelete and Wipe do not work under Windows 95, and long filenames can cause trouble.

✔ Scrolling down through a file using the DOWN ARROW key in **X-Tree Gold for Windows 4.0**, may cause GPFs. The work-around: use the mouse to scroll down through files instead of using the DOWN ARROW key.

Chapter 3 -- Windows 95 Hardware

Plug and Play went that-a-way!

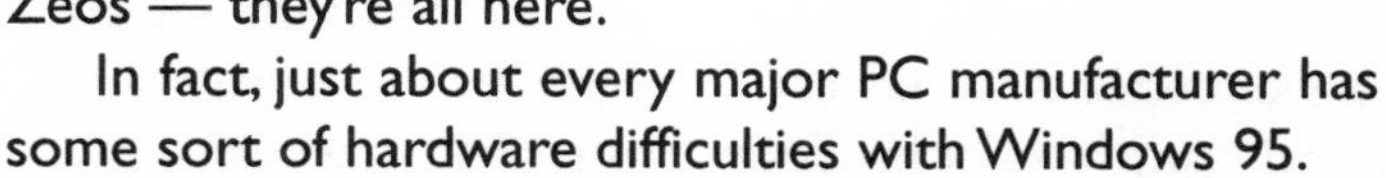

IBM, Compaq, Hewlett Packard, Toshiba, Gateway 2000, Dell, Canon, AST, DEC, NEC, Micron, Leading Edge, Zeos — they're all here.

In fact, just about every major PC manufacturer has some sort of hardware difficulties with Windows 95.

Most are relatively minor — if you know what to look out for — but there are also a few flat-out incompatibilities. As noted in our Installation chapter, for instance, you may not be able to install Windows 95 on some PCs running genuine Intel 386 CPUs.

Similarly, Iomega's PC2X 8-bit Bernoulli drive won't work on Pentiums running Windows 95, and neither will the Hewlett Packard 1300T Rewritable Optical Disk (with 1024-byte sectors) or the Orchid Vidiola video capture card.

The single greatest cause of bad chemistry between PC hardware and Windows 95, however, is actually software related — it's the drivers. In converting from a 16-bit to 32-bit system, Windows 95 necessarily threw many old hardware drivers into a cocked hat.

Although, interestingly, *sometimes* users of the older drivers have an advantage. For instance, at the time Windows 95 was released users of the new 32-bit PhotoShop 3.04 could not scan directly into the program with hardware like the Hewlett Packard ScanJet IIcx because PhotoShop couldn't use the old 16-bit TWAIN drivers, and there weren't any 32-bit TWAIN drivers for it yet.

However, users of the previous version of PhotoShop could merrily scan into the program all they wanted when running under Windows 95 because the old 16-bit drivers were available and still worked fine in this case. This momentarily gave people who hadn't upgraded a competitive advantage over those who had. In video land, the drivers situation is perhaps at its most chaotic. Here again, you'll see most of the big names -- like Diamond, ATI, Number 9, Orchid, and S3 -- represented.

CD-ROM drives by NEC are among those showing up with driver reports in this list, but perhaps the most anguished cries have come from users of that crucial business tool, the juke box CD-ROM multi-changer. When they installed Windows 95, these hipsters found they'd lost their juke boxes. Fortunately, there is a work-around which is detailed in the list that follows

All this may surprise people who thought that Microsoft's much touted Plug and Play technology would simplify hardware setup and maintenance. Microsoft proclaimed that Windows 95 would deliver "universal drivers" for printers, communications drivers, display adapter drivers, mouse drivers, and disk device drivers. Well, Plug

Bug/Fix Success Rates for Installation

The raw success rate for Windows 95 on Hardware related issues is a respectable 60 percent. This compares favorably with BugNet's data for non-Windows 95 problems during 1995.

Biggest Hardware Problem

This one is easy! In a word, it's drivers. Unfortunately, as of this writing, many companies have yet to release 32-bit protected mode drivers for Windows 95, which means that users are forced to make do with a patchwork of old and new. Better look before you leap.

Biggest Surprise

Communication speeds in some instances appear slower under Windows 95 than under Windows 3.1.

and Play is a great concept, but in fact Windows 95 suffers from problems in every one of these areas.

Most new Plug and Play devices work well (though not all, see the list that follows). Plug and Play even helps with the configuration of a good deal of legacy hardware, but the older, non-Plug and Play hardware sometimes still needs tweaking in the good old fashioned way. And in some cases, such as RGDI (Renaissance Graphics Device Interface), DGIS (Direct Graphics Interface Standard), and TIGA — there is no Windows 95 support at all.

Beyond drivers, Windows 95 seems to have difficulty with the advanced power management (APM) features on many laptops and "green" desktop PCs. Perhaps the eeriest of these is the problem with some "green" Gateway 2000 desktops which causes the cryptic error message, "time remaining unknown."

Ultimately, most of these problems will be ironed out, or the hardware will be left by the side of the road like armor on the retreat from Kuwait City.

It is also worth noting that people upgrading to Windows 95 probably need to worry more about these issues than people buying new Windows 95 machines.

Windows 95 Hardware Bug & Fix List

'Hail, Hail The Gang's All Here' and other favorites...

✔ When running Lotus **1-2-3 for Windows** and **CorelDRAW** under Windows 95, changing the imaging options (such as, "Print as a Negative Image," "Print as a Mirror Image," and "Compress Bitmap Images") through the PostScript printer driver may not work properly. The work-around: set these options through the application's print controls rather than the printer driver.

¥ When printing a Lotus **1-2-3 for Windows** spreadsheet that contains rotated text to a **Compaq PageMarq 20** printer at 800 x 400 resolution, the text may be rotated incorrectly. The work-around: change the graphics resolution to a symmetrical resolution such as 300 x 300.

Bug & Fix List Legend: The symbol ¥ denotes bugs, incompatibilities and other difficulties. The symbol ✔ denotes problems which have either been fixed, or resolved with some sort of acceptable work-around. Products are listed in alphabetical order.

✔ Here's a weird one. When trying to install Windows 95, you may get a page fault error if you have a Future Domain SCSI controller in your computer -- AND you may get one if you don't have a Future Domain SCSI controller installed in your computer. What gives? It turns out the problem has nothing to do with Future Domain. The problem is that you have **386Max** software installed, which makes the Adaptec ROM region read-only and causes the page fault error. The work-around: quit Setup, unload the 386Max software, and then run Setup again.

✔ Two-up or four-up printing (such as one would use in a brochure) does not work from Adobe **Acrobat Exchange 2.01** with the standard PostScript printer driver installed by Windows 95. The work-around is to revert to AdobePS driver 3.01 or later.

✔ If you change the 3D Objects color in the Display Properties dialog under Appearances, the activated buttons on Adobe **Acrobat Reader 2.1**'s toolbar will get strange. Adobe advises leaving the color settings alone.

✔ Your computer may freeze the first time it restarts after installing Windows 95 if you have an **Adaptec AIC-6360** SCSI chip which is disabled in your computer's CMOS settings. The work-around:

1. Start Windows 95 in Safe mode.
2. Use the right mouse button to click My Computer, then click Properties on the menu that appears.
3. On the Device Manager tab, double-click the SCSI Controller branch.
4. Click the SCSI adapter, then click Properties.
5. Click the Original Configuration check box to clear it, then click OK.

✔Windows 95 cannot detect or enumerate an **Adaptec 2940** SCSI controller installed on a PCI bus on computers with an AMI ROM BIOS version 1.00.07.AF2.The work-around: upgrade the AMI ROM BIOS to version 1.00.09.AF2.

✔ If you boot from a SCSI drive and have an **Adaptec 1542** SCSI controller, Windows 95 may not install the Windows 95 Protected Mode Adaptec SCSI driver, leaving the Real Mode driver intact. This slows performance to a crawl. According to Jason Levitt of Information Week, "You can force installation of the Windows 95 Protected Mode Adaptec SCSI driver by bypassing the Windows 95 hardware-detection phase and telling Windows 95 specifically to install the driver."

✔You may find you can't use the advanced power management (APM) features of your **AST Ascentia** 900N laptop computer with Windows 95. The work-around: configure Windows 95 to use APM version 1.0 instead of version 1.1:

1. Use the right mouse button to click My Computer, then click Properties on the menu that appears.
2. Click the Device Manager tab.
3. Click Advanced Power Management Support, then click Properties. Note that you may need to expand the System Devices branch of the hardware tree by double-clicking the branch, or by clicking the plus sign (+) to the left of the branch, before you can click Advanced Power Management Support.
4. Click the Settings tab.
5. Click the Force APM 1.0 Mode check box to select it.

✔ When printing from Windows 95 with some applications (e.g., Microsoft **Word for Windows**, Lotus **Ami** and **Road Atlas 4.0**) to a **Hewlett Packard DeskJet 1200c** or **PaintJet 300 XL** printer, you may find that colored or black text does not print on a colored or white background. The work-around is to use TrueType fonts and set your printer driver to print TrueType fonts as graphics. To print TrueType fonts as graphics, Microsoft advises:

1. Click the Start button on the taskbar.
2. On the Settings menu, click Printers.
3. Use the right (secondary) mouse button to click the HP DeskJet 1200c or PaintJet 300 XL printer icon, then click Properties.
4. Click the Fonts tab, then click the Print TrueType As Graphics check box.
5. Click OK to return to the Printers folder.

¥ Contrary to claims in its advertisements and mail solicitations, **Aracada Backup for Windows 95** will not work with all IDE tape drives. Contact Aracada to see if your drive is covered.

¥ The **AST** Plug and Play BIOS does not work properly with Windows 95, despite the name.

✔ If you use an **ATI Mach 8, Mach 32,** or **Mach 64** video card and Windows 95 is installed with the default 640 x 480 video resolution, you may find after you change the video resolution using the Change Display Type dialog box that Windows 95 still starts up with 640 x 480 resolution. The work-around: to use 800 x 600 or higher-resolution video mode with the ATI Mach 8, Mach 32, or Mach 64 video card, you must first configure the ATI card for the correct monitor type. This is done using the INSTALL.EXE program found on the disks provided with the ATI video adapters.

¥ If you use an **ATI Mach 64 ISA** display adapter in a Dell DE computer in which the onboard VGA adapter has been disabled through the CMOS rather than by using the jumper, your computer may freeze during Windows 95 Setup, or during detection if the ATI adapter is installed after Windows 95 is installed.

✔ With some **ATI Mach 64** video cards, when you change the display resolution in the Display Properties dialog box so that it is greater than 640 X 480 pixels and you select the 16 color option, the screen will become unreadable. The work-around: select the 256 color option for any resolution above 640 X 480 pixels.

✔ After you run the **ATI Mach32** setup utility (INSTALL.EXE), you may be unable to start the computer except in Safe Mode due to conflicts between ATI's Windows 3.1 drivers and Windows 95. The work-around: upgrade your drivers from ATI.

✔ If you are using an **ATI VGA Wonder XL24** display adapter and select the High Color (16-bit) or True Color (24-bit) color palette in the Display Properties dialog box, the system may start with garbled display. The work-around: restart your computer in safe mode, and then change the display mode to a lesser color depth, either 16 or 256 colors. To restart the computer in safe mode, do the following:

1. Click the Start button, click Shut down, and then click Restart The Computer.

2. When you see the message "Starting Windows 95," press the F8 key, and then select Safe Mode from the menu that appears.

¥ Iomega Technical Support has confirmed that the Iomega **PC2X 8-Bit Bernoulli** Controller card may not function properly on 486/33 MHz and faster computers running Windows 95. According to Microsoft, the work-around is to "use a slower computer or a different Bernoulli controller card."

✔ When printing to a **Canon LBP-81V** printer, the first few pages print correctly, but the remaining pages are blank. This problem can occur if the Canon LBP-81V printer is attached to the computer with a parallel cable more than 4 feet long. The blank pages occur because the Canon LBP-81V printer defaults to a 30-second time-out. Since this setting cannot be changed, the work-around is to use a parallel cable that is no more than four feet long.

¥ Although the **Canon LBP-8IV** printer supports printing 600 dpi when printing under Windows 3.1, the Windows 95 printer driver for this printer supports only 75, 150, or 300 dpi.

¥ When you click the Suspend command on the Start menu on a **Canon NoteJet II** 486C computer, the computer will not suspend, and when you use the computer's suspend button to suspend the computer, the computer suspends, but it will not resume. The work-around: don't suspend.

¥ If you have an older **Cirrus Logic** video card with a 5402 chip set (which is no longer manufactured or supported by Cirrus Logic), you can only use the Windows 95 standard VGA driver at less than 256 colors.

✔ If you get the error:

```
SUWIN caused a GPF in 256_1280.drv at
0002:0D7B.
```

when you upgrade from Windows version 3.1, the problem is probably that you have a **Cirrus Logic** Video Card driver installed on the computer which is incompatible with the Windows 95 Setup program. The work-around: restart the computer and run the Windows 95 Setup program from MS-DOS.

¥ If you have a VLB video adapter using the **Cirrus Logic** 5426, 5428, or 5434 video chip on a Pentium-based computer that has both VLB sockets and PCI sockets on the motherboard, you may find that the Windows 95 startup logo is distorted, and the interface appears in black and white during startup and while running Windows 95. The only work-around is to replace the VLB video adapter with a PCI adapter using the same chips, or a video adapter using a different video chip, such as the S3 or one manufactured by Tseng Labs.

¥ The **Clix** mouse is not fully functional in Windows 95. Use the standard mouse type to use the Clix mouse in two-button mode.

¥ If you install Windows 95 on a **Compaq Concerto** computer while it is docked, you may receive an

```
101-ROM Error
```

message when the computer restarts in the docking station. Contact Compaq for an updated BIOS which fixes the problem.

¥ The **Compaq Contura** Laptop computer and other Compaq computers using APM may tell you that battery status is high when in fact the battery is almost empty. The work-around: contact Compaq Corporation for information regarding an upgrade to the latest version of the APM BIOS.

✔ Physician heal thyself! If you install Windows 95 on a **Compaq Deskpro** that has a D:\ drive attached to a controller in an EISA slot, the first time you start the machine, the D:\ drive may be inaccessible. Fear not, however. The second time you start the computer and thereafter, the D:\ drive will work fine.

✔ When you are using the Media Pilot CD Sound System software installed on a **Compaq Presario** computer with Windows 95, audio CDs are incorrectly identified as data CDs. The work-around: to play an audio CD using the Media Pilot CD Sound System software in Windows 95, manually advance to the track you want, then click the Play button.

✔ If you try to "wake up" your **Compaq Presario 522, 524, 526** or **528** computer after Advanced Power Management (APM) has shut down the screen, the screen may remain in sleep mode. To re-activate the screen you must turn the computer off and back on. This apparently only occurs on units with the Cirrus Logic 54xxx video chip set. The work-around: do not enable APM in the computer's CMOS settings.

¥ With a **Compaq Presario CDS633**, if you select the High Color (16-bit) or True Color (24-bit) color palette in the properties for the display, the system may exit back to Standard VGA and prompt you to choose another display setting. The 16-bit and 24-bit color palettes may still be shown as available but you cannot actually use them. The work-around: Choose the 16 Color or 256 Color color palette. Also, you may want to contact Compaq for information about a possible video BIOS upgrade.

✔ When you are using Windows 95 on a **Compaq Summit 60** that supports Advanced Power Management (APM), you may find that nothing happens when you click the Suspend command on the Start menu. To disable the Suspend command on the Start menu:

1. Click the Start button, point to Settings, then click Control Panel.
2. Double-click the Power icon.
3. In the Show Suspend Command On Start Menu box, click the Never option button.

✔ If you are using **CorelSCSI** with Client for NetWare Networks, the LASTDRIVE statement added to CONFIG.SYS during CorelSCSI! setup may disable the mapped drives in the networks. The workaround: remove the LASTDRIVE statement.

¥ **CorelSCSI** does not support Windows 95. To get your CD-ROM to work, you need to disable CORELCDX, and try the version of MSCDEX that comes with Windows 95 instead.

✔ If you install Windows 95 on a **DEC Venturis** computer, you may find that Device Manager shows a Standard VGA node with a yellow exclamation point (!), and Windows 95 does not automatically detect or install any PCI or

ISAPNP adapters.The best solution is probably to contact DEC for an updated Plug and Play BIOS that is Windows 95 compatible.A BIOS date later than 6/1/95 should correct the problem.Alternatively, you can have Windows 95 recognize and configure PCI and ISAPNP devices correctly manually:

1. Click Settings, and then click Control Panel on the menu that appears.
2. Double-click the Add New Hardware icon.
3. In the Add New Hardware Wizard dialog box, click Next.
4. When asked "Do you want Windows to search for your new hardware?" click No, and Next.
5. Under Hardware types, click System devices, and then click Next.
6. Under Models, click PCI bus, click Next, and then continue through the Add New Hardware Wizard.

✔ If after you add a PCI device to your **Dell Dimension** computer the computer freezes, there is probably a conflict between the new PCI device and an existing legacy device, both of which are trying to use IRQ 10.The work-around: reconfigure the existing legacy device to use an IRQ other than IRQ 10.

✔ If you are using a **Diamond SpeedStar Pro VLB** video adapter, you may have trouble when you are using DriveSpace to compress an existing drive This can occur if the following line has been removed from your AUTOEXEC.BAT

```
C:\UTIL1\SPEED\PROMODE MONITOR
```

Microsoft notes that "this line is needed in order for the video adapter to support VGA mode in mini-Windows." The work-around:

1.Add PROMODE.EXE to the [FAILSAFE] section of the DRVSPACE.INF file.
2. Copy the PROMODE.EXE file to the fail-safe directory on the host drive.
3.Add a line in the AUTOEXEC.BAT file to load PROMODE.EXE and then restart the computer.

✔ After you install Windows 95 on a computer with a **Diamond Viper VLB** video card and the Diamond Windows 3.1 video drivers, you may find you can use only one setting. For example, you may only be able to use the 640 x 480 x 256 setting, or you may receive an error messages stating that the display adapter is not configured properly. To resolve this problem, Microsoft advises following these steps:
1. Click the Start button, point to Settings, then click Control Panel.
2. Double-click the System icon.
3. Click the Device Manager tab.
4. Double-click Display Adapters, click Standard Display Adapter (VGA), then click the Remove button. NOTE: Do not restart your computer when you are prompted to do so.
5. Use the Diamond Install tool in Control Panel to configure the resolution and colors.
6. Make sure the Viper environment variable SET statement in the AUTOEXEC.BAT file is correct.
7. Restart Windows 95.

¥ There are no Direct Draw drivers for Windows 95 written for the **Diamond Viper Pro** Video card yet. Because of this, there have been problems running AVI video files with this card.

¥ If you edit a text file in an MS-DOS command prompt session with the Windows 95 Edit tool, you may receive the error:

```
A fatal exception occurred at
0028:C0037E2E in VXD VDD(01) + 00001D8A.
The current application will be termi-
nated.
```

This error usually occurs if the MS-DOS command prompt window is maximized and you are using Windows 3.1 **Diamond Viper** video drivers. The only work-around is to use the Windows 95 standard VGA video driver, or obtain updated drivers from Diamond for the Viper video card.

✔ If you install the drivers for the **Diamond Sonic Sound LX** sound card, you may find that when you restart the computer you receive an error message stating that MMSYSTEM.DLL has changed, and/or you get no sound. The work-around: edit your SYSTEM.INI so that the line

```
WAVE=SND16
```

is changed to

```
WAVE=MMSYSTEM.DLL.
```

Also change the line

```
MIDI=SND16.DRV
```

to read

```
MIDI=MMSYSTEM.DLL
```

Then save and then close the file. Finally, extract the original MMSYSTEM.DLL to the Windows\System folder.

¥ No digital sound is available when you run Psygnosis **Diskworld** with a ESS688 sound card using an MS-DOS Prompt.

¥ When you check the status of your hard disk controller in Device Manager, you may see a red circle with a slash mark through it to the left of the controller, and the Animated Cursors may stop working. The problem may be that you have an incompatible version of the **E-Z Raid-1** controller card installed in your system. Another version of the controller card that came with Win32 drivers for Windows 3.1 is Windows 95 compatible.

¥ If you have a computer with a Cyrix CPU, such as an **Epson 866C** or **Microcenter Winbook**, you may experience periodic GPFs. To fix this problem you need to copy the file WB16OFF.EXE to your Windows directory. This is on the Windows 95 Setup Disk 1 (\WIN95 directory on CDROM). Then add the line:

```
C:\WINDOWS\WB16OFF.EXE
```

to your AUTOEXEC.BAT file.

¥ If you try to print to various Fargo Electronics printers (**Fargo Primera, PrimeraPro, Pictura, FotoFUN!**) you may find certain options in the Fargo printer drivers don't function properly. Contact Fargo for updated drivers.

¥ When using Spinnaker's PFS: **First Graphics** 1.0 with an ATI Mach32 Ultra Pro video adapter, 16-bit or 24-bit color settings may produce a monochrome display.

✔ Here's a weird one. When you run Windows 95 on a **Gateway 2000** desktop computer, a battery icon with a question mark on it may appear beside the clock on the taskbar and you may receive a warning message:

```
Time remaining unknown
```

This is due to the fact that some Gateway 2000 computers contain power-conservation features (they are sometimes known as "green machines"). These features resemble the advanced power management (APM) feature of portable

computers, confusing Windows 95. To disable the battery meter icon through the Control Panel:
1. Click the Start button, point to Settings, then click Control Panel.
2. Double-click the Power icon.
3. Click the Power tab, make sure the "Enable Battery Meter on Tray" check box is not selected.

¥ If Windows 95 does not recognize your machine as a Plug and Play computer even though you receive a message during startup that states
`Intel PnP BIOS Extensions Installed`
you may have one of the Intel-developed motherboards that are equipped with a Plug and Play BIOS but do not contain the run-time services necessary to configure motherboard devices. An example is the Intel 90 mhx Pentium that has shipped in machines from **Gateway 2000** and others. Consult your hardware vendor about upgrading your system BIOS to comply with the Plug and Play BIOS version 1.0a specification.

✔ To get **Gateway 2000**'s three-disk CD-ROM changers to work with Windows 95, you should:
1. Download SANYO3.VXD (available on the Gateway Forum on Compuserve) and copy it into your \WINDOWS\SYSTEM\IOSUBSYS directory.
2. Remove all references to CD-ROM or MSCDEX from your CONFIG.SYS and AUTOEXEC.BAT files.
3. Go Control Panel and right click on System, then Device Manager, then double click on Hard Disk Controllers. Scroll down the list and highlight the SECOND instance of IDE/ESDI controller. Then select Properties, and insure there is a check next to Current Configuration at the bottom of the screen, and click OK

3. Finally, shut down the system and reboot.

¥ Windows 95 Fax applet defaults to lower connection speeds than normal with USR, Intel 14.4, and **Gateway Telepath** modems. Microsoft claims this is to "ensure reliable transmissions," but this seems curious since one of the supposed promises was increased communication speeds over Windows 3.1.

✔ When you are installing Windows 95, you may receive a GPF after you accept the End User License Agreement if (1) your memory management software is incorrectly configured, (2) your computer has a **GSI BIOS**, or (3) double-buffering is required for your hard disk, but it is not enabled. The work-around(s): (1) configure the memory management software correctly; (2) contact your hardware vendor for information about possibly upgrading your GSI BIOS; or (3) enable double-buffering for your hard disk.

¥ **HardPC** (a hardware/software package designed to emulate MS-DOS on an Intergraph Clipper Workstation) is not compatible with Windows 95.

✔ **Harvard Graphics** 3.05 for DOS should be run in full-screen mode to avoid problems with a distorted display that can occur with the Diamond Stealth 64 (S3 chip set) video card.

¥ The **Hewlett Packard 1300T** Rewritable Optical Disk (with 1024-byte sectors) drive doesn't work properly with Windows 95 Backup.

✔When you try to change the video resolution on a **Hewlett Packard Vectra** computer running Windows 95, you may receive the following error message:

`There is a problem with your display settings. The adapter type is incorrect, or the current settings do not work with your hardware.`

The work-around: Run the HP Vectra's BIOS Setup program and change the display mode to an appropriate setting for the resolution you want to use. You may have to goof around a little to get it right.

You may not be able to play the audio tracks on some CD-ROM games on a **Hewlett Packard Vectra Communication** computer that incorporates a DSP-based combination sound/modem/fax/CD-ROM controller card. Some games (such as **Sound It Out Loud** by Conexus) do not progress beyond the opening screen. Other games may display error messages such as:

`MMSYSTEM 262 There is a problem with your media device. Make sure it is working properly or contact the device manufacturer.`

The work-around: try using the computer's original real-mode drivers, although doing so will degrade system performance somewhat:

1. Click the Start button, point to Settings, click Control Panel, and then double-click the System icon.
2. On the Device Manager tab, double-click the SCSI controller branch, and then double-click "Adaptec AIC-6x60 ISA Single Chip Controller."
3. Click the Original Configuration (Current) check box to clear it, and click OK.
4. Add the following lines to the CONFIG.SYS:

```
device=c:\hp_iobrd\adaptec\aspi2dos.sys
device=c:\hp_iobrd\adaptec\aspicd.sys /
d:aspicd0
```

5. Remove the semicolon from the beginning of the MSCDEX entry and then save and close the CONFIG.SYS.
6. Add the following line to the AUTOEXEC.BAT:

```
c:\windows\command\mscdex.exe /d:aspicd0
```

(NOTE: you may have to goof with this line a little to get it to work on your machine.)
7. Restart your computer.

✔ If you get an

```
Error 21
```

message when printing to a **Hewlett-Packard LaserJet 4** under Windows 95, try changing the graphics mode from Vector to Raster.

✔ After you receive an "Out of paper" message and refill the paper tray on a **Hewlett Packard DeskJet 560c,** the printer still may not print. Clicking Retry in the message box only repeats the message. To start the printer if this occurs, you need to press the Load/Eject button on the printer. The job, and any subsequent jobs, then will print.

✔ When you print a selected map from the **Microsoft Bookshelf '94 Atlas** to a **Hewlett-Packard LaserJet III** or **IIISi**, the printed map appears to contain dots or dithering which are not apparent when you print from Windows version 3.1. The work-around: set the Windows 95 dithering option for the HP LaserJet III or IIISi to None. Here's how:

1. Click the Start button, Settings, and then Printers.
2. Use the right (secondary) mouse button to select the HP LaserJet III or IIISi printer.

3. Click Properties, then click the Graphics tab.
4. Under Dithering, click None, then OK.

✔The printer driver setup program for the **Hewlett Packard DeskJet** family of printers may fail under Windows 95, or you may not be able to print to your DeskJet printer because the Hewlett Packard printer driver setup program, HPSETUP, is not compatible with Windows 95. The work-around: use the DeskJet printer driver that ships with Windows 95.

✔ New 32-bit PCL drivers, versions 30.445 for **OS/2** and **Hewlett Packard** printers, are available in Library 2 of the Hewlett-Packard Forum on CompuServe .(GO HPPER) The file name is MP240EN.EXE, and has a date of 9/16/95.

✔The Windows 95 driver for **Hewlett Packard JetAdmin 2.01.55** is now available in the JetDirect and Network library of the Hewlett Packard CompuServe forum. The file is called JA95UP.EXE and is dated 9/17/95.

✔ If you are having tray-selection problems with a **Hewlett Packard 5P** printer working under Windows 95, sysop Deanne Payne of the Hewlett Packard Forum on CompuServe reports that some users are getting good results using the LaserJet 4+ drivers.

✔ If you have a problem with blank pages printing before your print job on a **Hewlett Packard DeskJet 540**, Peter Railton of West Brisbane, Australia, has solved it by copying LPT.VDX from the CD version on Windows 95 in the DRIVERS\PRINTER\LPT\ directory to his WINDOWS\SYSTEM directory.

¥ There have been numerous complaints with the **Hewlett Packard DeskJet 6xx** printers in Windows 95. The Hewlett Packard sysops have suggested using either the 550c or 1200c drivers until a 6xx driver is released. However, this fix is not working for everyone.

✔ If you get an extra page at the end of print jobs with error messages like

```
"%-12345x@PJL
@PJL JOB NAME = "MSJOB 1"
@PJL USTATUS JOB = ON
@PJL USTATUS PAGE = OFF
@USTATUS DEVICE = ON
@PJL USTATUS TIMED = 0
```

on it when trying to print to a **Hewlett Packard LaserJet 4**, the problem may be solved by copying the file LPT.VDX from your Windows 95 CD-ROM (you'll have to have the ShowAll option selected in Options off the Tools menu in Explorer or a folder window to be able to see the file) to your WINDOWS\SYSTEM directory.

✔ To successfully run **Hewlett Packard ScanJet** scanner with Windows 95, the key is to make sure you use version 2.2 of the **DeskScan II** software. According to Annie Baxter, sysop on Compuserve's Hewlett Packard Peripheral Forum, "My understanding is that Win16 applications (such as Adobe PhotoShop 2.5, and Corel Photo-Paint 5.0) will be able to do a TWAIN acquire using the DeskScan software, but TWAIN32 applications (such as Adobe Photoshop 3.0) will not." Version 2.2 is available as SJ195EN.EXE in lib 11 (ScanJet) of the Hewlett Packard Peripheral Forum.

✔ If you try to re-install or upgrade the copy of Windows 95 on an **IBM Aptiva 710,** you may receive the following error:

```
Setup: Error SU0507
The following problem occurred while
Setup was analyzing your computer:
SDMErr(8037001b): Detection function
returned a DMS error.
DMSError: This computer cannot be up-
graded from Windows. Please shutdown
Windows and upgrade in MS-DOS mode.
```

The work-around: restart your computer in MS-DOS mode and then run Setup. If you receive a GPF, Microsoft says you should "ignore the error message and continue."

✔ If you boot to a real-mode MS-DOS command prompt and install Windows 95 over an existing Windows 95 installation on an **IBM ThinkPad** computer, your computer may freeze when you try to start Windows 95. According to Microsoft, "this problem occurs only if you install Windows 95 from a network server and you are using a PCMCIA network adapter to access the network." The work-around: run Windows 95 Setup from the graphical user interface (GUI) rather than from a real-mode MS-DOS command prompt.

¥ The detection routine in Windows 95 Setup does not detect the PCMCIA socket in **IBM ThinkPad 720C** computers. The PCMCIA socket also is not detected when you run the Add New Hardware Wizard from Control Panel. As a result, protected-mode socket services are not provided. To use the PCMCIA socket on an IBM ThinkPad

720C, you must install the real-mode socket drivers using the manufacturer's instructions.

✔ On the **IBM ThinkPad 750 and 750C**, PCMCIA cards appear twice under the Device Manager card class. To eliminate this redundancy:

1. Click the Start button, point to Settings, then click Control Panel.
2. Double-click the System icon, and then click the Device Manager tab.
3. Expand the PCMCIA Socket branch and click "Intel PCIC Compatible PCMCIA Controller."
4. Click the Properties button, then click the Socket Services tab.
5. In the Number Of Sockets box, change the value from Automatic Detection to 2.
6. Click Apply Now on all open property sheets, then click Shut Down on the taskbar and restart Windows 95.

✔ If you are using an **IBM ThinkPad 755, 750, 360, Toshiba T4800, T4850, T4700** (or any other machine with a Western Digital 90C24A controller), you may see a horizontal strip running across the screen when you open a full-screen MS-DOS session and then press CTRL+ESC to switch back to the Windows 95 graphic user interface. The work-around:

1. Click Settings, then click Control Panel.
2. Double-click the System icon.
3. On the Performance tab, click Graphics.
4. Move the Hardware Acceleration slider one notch to the left, and click OK.

✔ When you are installing Windows 95 on an **IBM ThinkPad** computer, Setup may freeze while detecting hardware in the computer if you have a video capture device installed. The work-around: run Setup again and choose the Safe Recovery option when you are prompted. Repeat this process as many times as are necessary to complete Setup.

✔ When you print from **Windows 95 WordPad** on an **IBM 4019PS17**, the underscore character (_) in the PostScript printer font Courier does not print. The work-around: print the document using the Windows 95 Courier New TrueType font.

¥ The version 4.0 drivers for the **J-Mouse** features of the Sejin J.M. Keyboard are not compatible with Windows 95, according to Microsoft.

¥ When you try to open the Printers folder from the Settings menu, Control Panel, My Computer, or Windows Explorer, you receive the following error message:

```
Not enough storage to complete this
operation.
```

if you are using a LaserMaster printer driver. The **LaserMaster LX8 600** dots per inch (DPI) LaserJet add-on controller card does not work with Windows 95, and LaserMaster has confirmed that it will not provide updated drivers for the LX8 LaserJet add-on controller card. There is no work-around at this time.

✔ When you are installing Windows 95 on a **Leading Edge Fortiva 5000**, you may receive an error like:

```
Missing Operating System
```

or

```
Invalid System Disk
```

after which the computer will no longer boot from the hard drive. The work-around:

1. Restart your computer using the Emergency Startup Disk.

2. Use the SYS command to transfer system files to the hard disk. For example, if the Emergency Startup Disk is in drive A, type the following line:

```
sys c:
```

3. Then remove the Emergency Startup Disk from the floppy disk drive, restart your computer and continue Setup.

✔ If you run the Microsoft Windows 95 Setup program from an MS-DOS prompt on a computer with a **Logitech mouse** installed, the mouse may not function until Setup has restarted the computer to boot Windows 95, unless you start Windows 95 Setup with the command
SETUP /IL

✔ When you try to start **Master Tracks 4 Professional 4.9**, you may receive the following error message

```
Unable to run the program. This is a USE
version, please contact your Passport
dealer.
```

followed by an error message from Windows 95:

```
This program has performed an illegal
operation and will be shut down. If the
problem persists, contact the program
vendor.
```

To correct this problem, upgrade to the later version of Master Tracks 4 Professionals.

✔ If you try to install the Windows 3.1 drivers for your **Media Vision MV-1100** sound card and then restart your computer, you will receive an error message stating that the MCICDA.DRV, MMMIXER.DLL, and MSMIXER.DLL files have been replaced with older versions and that you should run Setup again. If you don't run run Setup, but instead restart Windows 95, you receive a GPF, and afterwards Windows 95 will only start in Safe mode. This happens because the Media Vision Deluxe Windows 3.1 drivers are not compatible with Windows 95. The workaround: start Windows 95 in Safe mode, and then run Setup again to reinstall Windows 95 over the existing installation, choosing the option to replace only corrupted files.

✔ When you use the Shut Down command to shut down Windows 95 on a **Micron Pentium 90-MHz** computer, the computer may freeze because its BIOS (revision number 4.04 M54Pi-N14p) is incompatible with Windows 95. Contact Micron for an upgrade.

✔ In Caere **Wordscan Plus 3.0**, errors can occur during scanning if **Microtek ScanMaker IIsp** with the supplied SCSI 2 card and WordScan Plus 3.0 is selected in the WordScan scanner setup dialog box. To avoid problems, select the TWAIN scanner in the scanner setup dialog box.

✔ After installing Windows 95, you may find that you can not scan into **PhotoShop 3.04** with a **Microtek ScanMaker II/IIxe, IIsp, IIg, IIhr, III, or 35t**. To rectify the situation, you should download Microtek TWAIN Scan Module version 1.73 (available in Library 6 in Compuserve's Graphsupport Forum at TW173R1.EXE). Then you should install the new TWAIN driver, and probably reinstall PhotoShop and accept the default directory (C:\WIN32APPS\PHOTOSHOP). Ed Moon of Microtek also suggets putting the ~\windows\twain directory on the DOS path in your AUTOEXEC.BAT. Alternatively, you can use another program (such as CorelPaint 6) to make your scans.

✔ **Mustek Paragon MFS-6000CX** Flatbed Scanner will only operate with the supplied proprietary SCSI-2 card. Third party SCSI controllers won't work.

✔ If your computer freezes when you try to use an audio CD in a **NEC Intersect CDR-37** CD-ROM drive, and ejecting the CD causes the error message
`Drive Not Ready`
and you can use the system normally once you close the error message box, the problem is that the drive does not support Windows 95's protected mode drivers. However, the drive should function correctly with audio CDs when you are using real-mode CD-ROM and MSCDEX.EXE drivers. To use real-mode drivers instead of the Windows 95 protected-mode drivers, load the CD-ROM driver in the CONFIG.SYS file, and load MSCDEX.EXE in the AUTOEXEC.BAT file following the manufacturer's instructions. Note that if these drivers were already installed when you installed Windows 95, they may still be in the CONFIG.SYS and AUTOEXEC.BAT files, but be remarked out. If using the real-mode drivers does not resolve the problem, you may need to disable the CD-ROM drive in Device Manager.

✔ **NEC IDE CD-ROM** drives may not run under Windows 95. The work-around: use real-mode CD-ROM drivers for the CD-ROM drive.

✔ When you try to start your **NEC Powermate 466** for the first time after installing Windows 95, you may receive the following:

```
Windows Protection Error
```

The work-around: restart Windows 95 using the Command Prompt Only option on the Startup menu. Run Setup again, with the following command:

```
setup /p i
```

✔ If you encounter difficulties printing from PageMaker 5 to the **NEC SuperScript 610**, contact NEC for the latest drivers, which solve the problems.

✔ When you double-click the Power icon in Control Panel on a **NEC Versa**, you may receive the following error message:

```
RUNDLL32 Caused a General Protection
Fault in APMEXT.DLL
```

The work-around: remove the following line from the [Power.drv] section of the System.ini file, and then restart Windows 95:

```
OptionsDll=apmext.dll
```

¥ The output of the **Okidata OL-410ex** printer may be garbled at 600 dots per inch under Windows 95. Microsoft advises: "Verify that Windows 95 is configured to use the proper printer driver for the printer you are using. If you are using the correct printer driver, change the print resolution to 300 dpi or upgrade the printer to 2 MB or more of memory."

✔ Using an **Orchid Celsius VLB** video card and version 1.1 drivers with Windows 95, you may find your computer freezes in 1024 x 768 x 256 mode. Also, when you start

Windows 95 in Safe mode, you may get the following error:

```
Explorer executed an invalid instruction
in module shell32.dll at 0137:79342eb.
```

In addition, if you try as a last resort to use Windows 95's standard VGA display driver to use with this video card, small rectangular boxes appear on the screen at random after the screen is redrawn. The reason is that the Orchid Windows 3.x video drivers do not work properly with Windows 95. The work-around: install the XGA video drivers provided with Windows 95, using one of the following resolutions: 640 x 480 x 8 BPP (256 colors), 640 x 480 x 16 BPP (65536 colors), 800 x 600 x 8 BPP (256 colors), 800 x 600 x 16 BPP (65536 colors), 1024 x 768 x 4 BPP (16 colors), 1024 x 768 x 8 BPP (256 colors -- interlaced or 72-Hz monitor types).

¥ Windows 95 detects and configures the **Orchid Vidiola** video capture card as a Vidiola Standard card. There is no work-around at present that doesn't create other problems. Microsoft advises that you contact Orchid for help.

✔ If you have a STB (S3 based) video card, Alarm related GPF's in **Organizer 2.1** may be cured by updating the video driver. The good driver is P6421C.ZIP, dated 7/28/95, and can be found in the Graphics A Vendors Forum on CompuServe, in the STB section.

¥ When you print a file that includes a TIFF image from Adobe **PageMaker 5.0** to a **QMS 860** PostScript printer, you may get an error like:

```
Error: undefined
Offending Command: colorimage
```

The problem is that PageMaker defaults to Postscript level 2 output and the QMS 860 is a Postscript level 1 device. There is no work-around at present.

¥ If you are printing from **PageMaker 5** to a **Hewlett Packard LaserJet 4** using Microsoft's Windows 95 drivers, you may find that you can print 99 copies of a document, but not 100.

✔ When opening documents created with **PageMaker 5** running under **Windows 3.1**, you may get an error message like:

```
cannot load driver for HP Laserjet 4p/
4pm on LPT1
```

even if you have the appropriate printer driver installed on your system. The problem is that Windows 95 uses different names for the drivers, and therefore is confused by old driver references. The work-around: load the document, re-compose for the printer in question, then save the document. You may have to do this the first time you open every old PageMaker document in Windows 95, but after that everything should be OK.

✔ You may find that you are unable to get more than 300 DPI when printing from **PageMaker 5** to a **Hewlett Packard LaserJet 4**. To get back to full 600 DPI output, you should first check your printer driver settings, because Microsoft's Windows 95 driver seems to default to 300 DPI. If the problem persists, you should download and install LJWIN3.ZIP from Hewlett Packard's Compuserve Forum. You're not out of the woods yet, though. You next must open the Printer Folder, click on the icon for your new driver, and, under the dropdown File Menu, select "Select as Default Printer." When you open PageMaker again, voila!, there you should see verification that you are set up for 600 DPI.

✔ When you are creating a Startup Disk during Windows 95 Setup, you may get error messages like:

`Disk Initialization Error`

or

`Could not properly initialize the floppy disk that you inserted.`

or

`Error: Disk sector was not found.`

if the floppy disk drive in your computer is connected to a **Promise IDE** controller. The work-around: don't create a Startup Disk during Setup. Instead, create a Startup Disk after Setup is finished. To do this:

1. Click the Start button, point to Settings, and then click Control Panel.
2. Double-click the Add/Remove Programs icon.
3. Click the Startup Disk tab, and then the Create Disk button.

¥ When you are setting up Windows 95, the mouse attached to your computer may be incorrectly identified as a **PS/2**-style or an Inport (bus) mouse, and as a result the mouse won't work. The reason, according to Microsoft, is that "setup detects mouse ports in the following order: Inport, PS/2, serial. When the detection routine finds the mouse port, it stops searching. For example, if Setup finds an Inport card, it stops searching for the mouse." The work-around? If you have an Inport card, remove the card from the computer before you run Setup. If you have a PS/2-style mouse port, you may be out of luck. Contact your computer vendor about a possible BIOS upgrade (always fun!).

✔ If you are using **QEMM** and an older S3 video adapter, your computer may freeze when you start Windows 95. The work-around: remove or disable the following line in your CONFIG.SYS, and then restart your computer:

```
device=c:\qemm\loadhi.sys /r:1
c:\qemm\qdpmi.sys swapfile=dpmi.swp
```

or use 16-color mode.

✔ After Windows 95 automatically detects your **Racal** modem, the modem may stop working because Windows 95 sends the command "AT%V" to the modem, which switches the modem off (nice trick). The work-around: reset the modem by turning your computer off and back on.

✔ When you are using an **S3** video adapter with any resolution with more than 256 colors, the mouse pointer may disappear.

The work-around:

1. Click the Start button, point to Settings, then click Control Panel.
2. Double-click the System icon.
3. On the Performance tab, click Graphics.
4. Move the Hardware Accelerator slider one notch to the left (to the Most Accelerator Functions setting) and click OK.

✔ When you are using a High Color resolution (with more than 256 colors) with an **S3** video card, the colors on the screen may have a blue tint. The work-around: add the following line to the [display] section of your SYSTEM.INI and then restart your computer:

```
HighColor=15
```

✔ When you are using an **S3 911/924** video adapter, text on the screen may appear as a series of blocky characters if you use a color cursor. The work-around: use only a black and white cursor.

¥ According to Microsoft, **ScanMan Color Handheld Scanner with ScanMan Software for Images 1.1** & **FotoTouch Color 1.10** from Logitech won't work if the computer has more than 20MB RAM.

✔ During Setup, the **Sony CD-ROM** drive in your computer may not be detected if it is attached to a MediaVision sound card. The work-around: set up the Sony CD-ROM drive in Windows 95 manually. You will need to know the CD-ROM drive's settings to do this. Please contact Sony.

✔ Windows 95 may freeze when you press CTRL+ALT+DEL to reboot and then try to use the **Sound Blaster** or **MediaVision Pro Audio SCSI CD-ROM** drive. The work-around: use the reset button instead of CTR+ALT+DEL.

✔ Windows 95 does not detect the **STB Lightspeed Tseng 4000 W32p** PCI video adapter as a PCI card because early revisions of the W32p chip were not strictly PCI compatible. Therefore the video adapter does not report itself as a PCI card. Performance of the video adapter is unaffected, however.

¥ Zenographics **SuperPrint 2.0** (or earlier) for Windows does not run correctly under Windows 95.

¥ Windows 95 may not recognize **Sound It Out Loud 2** from Conexus If your computer uses a **TEAC 55a** CD drive.

✔ When printing to the **Texas Instruments MicroLaser Pro 600 PS23** PostScript printer, you may find that the data light on the printer blinks as the page is received, but there is no output, or part of the page is garbled, or the printer prints the error message:

```
Restarted due to fatal system error at
address 0X9FD100E4
```

You should contact Texas Instruments about a possible firmware upgrade for the printer. This problem does not occur with firmware version 2014.105 rev. 22 b and higher.

✔ When you use the Suspend command on Windows 95's Start menu on a **Toshiba 4500** computer, the machine may spontaneously restart during the resume phase. The work-around: suspend by using the Suspend button on the portable computer rather than by using the Suspend command on Windows 95's Start menu, or contact Toshiba for an updated APM.SYS driver.

✔ If you shut down a **Toshiba 4500** laptop running Windows 95 in Suspend mode or close the lid, Windows 95 may appear to shut down successfully, but when you resume Windows 95, the computer will soon spontaneously reboot. The work-around: obtain the RESUME.386 file from Toshiba, and then add it to your SYSTEM.INI.

✔ After you change the video resolution on a **Toshiba T3100** computer to a resolution higher than 256 colors, the screen may go black when you restart Windows 95.

The reason is that the built-in screen on the Toshiba T3100 computer does not support more than 256 colors, even though it supports 64,000 (16-bit) colors when connected to an external moniter. The work-around is:

1. Restart the computer.
2. When you see the "Starting Windows 95" message, press the F5 key to start Windows 95 in Safe mode.
3. Change the video resolution to 256 colors or less.
4. Restart Windows 95 normally.

✔ If you use the Audio Control (AUDCNTRL.EXE) utility that ships with the **Toshiba T4800CT**, you may find that when you minimize an application, it does not minimize to the taskbar; instead, the icon disappears. The work-around: even though you can't see the icon, you can still use your ALT+TAB key combination to cycle through running applications, and select the one you want.

¥ According to Stephen Feldman of Toshiba, there are a number of problems with the suspend function with Windows 95 and **Toshiba notebooks** (and notebooks in general); he suggests keeping the notebook system in boot mode and temporarily disabling the Autoresume function letting Windows 95 control this capability.

✔ When you install Windows 95 on a NEC Image P90E computer, Setup may not detect a **Tseng ET4000/W32** PCI video adapter in the computer. If so, Windows 95 Setup installs the standard VGA display driver. The work-around: manually select the Tseng ET4000/W32 video adapter. (NOTE: Make sure you don't select the ET4000/W32 PCI video adapter.)

✔ If Windows 95 Setup detects more than one floppy disk drive controller when you only have one, the problem may be that you have the **Ultrastor 24F EISA SCSI** adapter. Contact Ultrastor about upgrading the 24F controller to a 24Fa controller. Or, if you're bold, you can try this work-around. First, using the EISA configuration utility, set the floppy disk drive controller as the primary controller. (The default is disabled.) Now remove the JP7 jumper on the board.

¥ Microsoft Windows 95 does not have the capability to print to a printer on a machine running **UNIX** only. However, if the printer is on a Microsoft **Windows NT 3.5** server or a Novell **NetWare** server that is also running UNIX, Microsoft says you should be able to print to it.

✔ Windows 95 may not detect the **U.S. Robotics Courier V.34** fax/modem installed in your computer. The work-around: obtain an updated flash BIOS dated later than 7/5/95 from U.S. Robotics.

✔ When you use a **U.S. Robotics Sportster 28.8** modem in Windows 95, it may begin to drop characters or bits after long use, resulting in corrupted files and garbled messages. U.S. Robotics has confirmed that Sportster 28.8 modems with a firmware revision prior to 4/18/95 can experience this problem. The problem affects internal, external, and PCMCIA modems. The work-around: obtain a firmware revision dated 4/18/95 or later from U.S. Robotics.

✔ When you are installing Windows 95 on a computer using Viva Computers' **VITEX RS232 (HMC83451) serial card**, the mouse may freeze after Setup finishes its hardware detection if the mouse is installed on COM1. The work-around: install the mouse on COM2.

✔ After you use the **Vortek Utilities** SET RES tool to change the display resolution and Windows 95 restarts your computer, you may receive the following error message:

```
Error in EXE file
```

The work-around: restart your computer and boot to a command prompt by pressing the F8 key when you see the "Starting Windows 95" message. Choose "Command Prompt Only" when you are prompted. Then, replace your (probably damaged) WIN.COM file by extracting the WIN.CNF file from the original Windows 95 disks or CD-ROM.

✔ The **Wacom** pen tablet attached to your computer may not function correctly after you install Windows 95. The work-around: reinstall the software included with the Wacom pen tablet.

✔ If the right mouse button does not bring up any menu or dialog boxes, or nothing happens at at all when the right mouse button is clicked, you may correct the problem by going into the mouse setup under **Windows 95** and changing it to Assigned.

✔ If the bottom portion of **Windows 95's CD Player** is off the screen or inaccessible., the problem is probably that the font has somehow gotten set to 16 pt or higher. To correct this:

1. Right click an empty area on the desktop, and then click Properties on the menu that appears.
2. Click the Appearance tab, then Menu

3. Change the font size to 16 or less, or increase the menu size, click OK

¥ Left-handed operation settings established in **Windows 95** are inaccessible to the user when running MS-DOS-based programs in full-screen mode. You can use them, however, when running MS-DOS programs in a Window.

¥ If you receive frequent
`Parity Error`
messages on a blue screen in **Windows 95**, forcing you to restart your computer, Microsoft advises that the problem may be caused by defective memory chips in the computer.

¥ If one of your PCI devices in Device Manager shows an
`error code 29`
the problem according to Microsoft is that "**Windows 95** requires that a disabled PCI device has its IRQ written in the PCI configuration space by the BIOS. If the BIOS does not enable the card and does not give it an IRQ, Windows 95 shows an error code 29 because Windows 95 cannot enable the device without an IRQ and Windows 95 cannot assign a PCI device an IRQ." The work-around: contact your computer manufacturer to find out if there is a way to enable the card and give it an IRQ.

After installing Microsoft Mouse driver version 9.0 or 9.01 in **Windows 95**, you may receive the following error:

```
Cannot find a device file that may be
needed to run Windows or a Windows ap-
plication. The Windows registry or
System.ini file refers to this device
file, but the device file no longer
exists. If you deleted this file on
```

```
purpose, try uninstalling the associated
application using its uninstall or Setup
program. If you still want to use the
application associated this device file,
try reinstalling that application to
replace the missing file.
```

When you press a key, you receive the following error message:

```
Error loading C:\mouse\mouse.drv. You
must reinstall Windows.
```

The work-around: manually update your SYSTEM.INI and WIN.INI:

1. Restart the computer. When you see the "Starting Windows 95" message, press the F8 key and then choose Command Prompt Only from the Startup menu.
2. In your SYSTEM.INI change the line that reads:

```
mouse.drv=c:\mouse\mouse.drv
```

to read:

```
mouse.drv=mouse.drv
```

3. Change the line that reads

```
keyboard=C:\mouse\mousevkd.386
```

or

```
keyboard=C:\msinput\msinput.386
```

to read:

```
keyboard=*vkd
```

4. Save your SYSTEM.INI and then open your WIN.INI.
5. Remove the following entry from the "load=" line:

```
C:\mouse\pointer.exe
```

or

```
C:\msinput\pointer.exe
```

(Do not remove any other entry from the "load=" line.)

6. Save and close the file.
7. Restart Windows 95 normally.

8. Press ALT+S, use the UP ARROW key to select Settings, press the RIGHT ARROW key to select Control Panel, and then ENTER.
9. Select the Mouse tool, and then press ENTER.
10. Select the General tab.
11. Press ALT+C.
12. Press ALT+A to show all devices, and then select an appropriate mouse driver from the list.
13. After you press the OK button, restart your computer when you are prompted.

✔ Although **Windows 95** supports jukebox type CD-ROM changers, Microsoft advises that the best results will be obtained by using real-mode — rather than protected-mode — CD-ROM drivers (if you are loading a CD-ROM driver in your CONFIG.SYS file and MSCDEX in your AUTOEXEC.BAT file, you are using real-mode drivers).

✔ When using a jukebox type CD-ROM changers with **Windows 95** supports, you may experience long delays when performing shell operations such as querying the system (for example, whenever you run My Computer or Explorer). The length of this delay depends on the number of CDs in the changer. One work-around is to set up a large CD-ROM cache (if you have a ton of physical RAM); another is to use real-mode drivers.

✔ If you install **Windows 95** on a system with two CD-ROM drives, the second CD may not be recognized by Windows 95. The situation occurs when Windows 95 loads a protected mode driver for one CD-ROM drive, and the other retains the original real-mode driver (loaded in the CONFIG.SYS and AUTOEXEC.BAT files). Microsoft explains: Although Windows 95 supports jukebox type CD-

ROM changers, Microsoft advises that the best results will be obtained by using real-mode — rather than protected-mode — CD-ROM drivers (if you are loading a CD-ROM driver in your CONFIG.SYS file and MSCDEX in your AUTOEXEC.BAT file, you are using real-mode drivers). Microsoft explains: "Windows 95 assumes that the real-mode and protected-mode drivers reference the exact same drive; therefore, it assigns the drive letter for the protected-mode drive to be the same as the existing real-mode drive letter." To assign a new drive letter:

1. Click the Start button, point to Settings, and then click Control Panel.
2. Double-click the System icon, then click the Device Manager tab.
3. Select the CD-ROM you want to change from the list, then click the Properties button.
4. Choose the Settings tab.
5. In the Reserved Drive Letters section, set Start Drive Letter and End Drive Letter to the drive letter you want the CD-ROM to use.
6. Click the Start button on the taskbar and click Shut Down. Then restart your Computer.

¥ **Windows 95** does not provide specific drivers for RGDI (Renaissance Graphics Device Interface), DGIS (Direct Graphics Interface Standard), or TIGA. When Setup is detecting the installed hardware, it detects these cards as VGA.

✔ You will not be able to resize an MS-DOS-based application's window in **Windows 95** using the mouse if you have enabled the Exclusive Mode option for the application's mouse settings. To disable the Exclusive Mode option:

1. Press ALT+ENTER to switch the application to run in a full screen.
2. Press ALT+TAB until the application is minimized.
3. Use the right mouse button to click the application's button on the taskbar and then click Properties on the menu that appears.
4. Choose the Misc tab.
5. In the Mouse section, click the Exclusive Mode check box to clear it.

¥ When you are running **Windows 95** on a notebook computer that supports Advanced Power Management (APM), the Suspend command on the Start menu may not work properly when the notebook computer is plugged into an external power source. The work-around: modify your computer's BIOS settings to enable APM functionality while the computer is connected to an external power source. Please refer to the computer's documentation for specific instructions.

✔ In **Windows 95** Microsoft acknowledges that "When you perform a warm undocking operation for a portable computer docked to a main computer that is connected to a network and is running Microsoft Exchange Mail Client, the computer seems to stop responding (hangs), generates a general protection fault, or generates another type of fatal error." The work-around: close Microsoft Exchange, perform the docking operation, and then restart Microsoft Exchange.

¥ When **Windows 95** is loading you may receive the following error:

```
An error occurred while trying to ini-
tialize the video adapter.
```

and CTRL+ALT+DEL does reboot the system. To correct this problem, change your video driver back to the default Windows 95 VGA setting. To change your video driver back to VGA:

1. Click the Start button, point to Settings, then click Control Panel.
2. Double-click the Display icon.
3. Choose the Settings tab.
4. Click the Change Display Type button, then click the Change button for Adapter Type.
5. Click Standard Graphics Adapter (VGA), then click OK. When asked whether to use the current driver or a new driver, click Current.

✔You may receive GPFs in various applications running under **Windows 95** if you are using a Windows version 3.1 video driver that supports bitmaps. The work-around is to use one of the video drivers supplied with Windows 95 (such as the standard VGA driver), or disable bitmap support on your video card.

¥ It is impossible to create a bootable floppy for **Windows 95** on a 360K disk because the system files require 422K of disk space.

¥ In **Windows 95** Explorer, there is no method to move the vertical bar that divides the directory tree and file-listing window without a mouse. Similarly, when you are viewing a window in Details mode, there is no option to change the size of the fields for the file Name, Type, Total Size, and Free Space listings. You also cannot use the right mouse button to click the small icon in the upper left corner of the title bar to display the context menu for a folder. Nor can you start the Media Player VCR control buttons without a mouse.

¥ When you use the SUBST command on a removable drive, you do not have access to the substituted drive in **Windows 95** (not even at an MS-DOS prompt within Windows 95).

✔ If the Device Manager displays an exclamation point in a yellow circle for a PCI device, and a status message like:

```
The device has been disabled in the
hardware. In order to use this device,
you must re-enable the hardware. See
your hardware documentation for details.
(Code 29.)
```

the problem may be that **Windows 95** knows the hardware will not function, or the hardware is configured incorrectly. Microsoft advises: "You may be able to resolve the problem by removing the device and refreshing it on the PCI bus. This causes the PCI bus to be enumerated again and lets Windows 95 reconfigure the hardware. To remove and refresh a PCI device, follow these steps:

1. Click the Start button, point to Settings, then click Control Panel.
2. Double-click the System icon.
3. Click the Device Manager tab, click the PCI device, then click the Remove button.
4. Click the View Devices By Connection option button and then click PCI Bus.
5. Click the Refresh button."

✔ After **Windows 95** reboots at the completion of Setup, you may receive the following error:

```
Missing operating system
```

if you have a DISCTEC removable hard disk drive set as the boot drive. The work-around (if Windows 95 is already installed on your system):

1. Boot your computer with a bootable floppy disk.
2. Insert the DISCTEC installation disk in the floppy disk drive and change to this drive (A: or B:).
3. Use DISCTEC's hard disk drive partitioning software to rewrite the partition table as follows:

```
HDPRT /w /0
```

(The last character above is a zero.)

4. Reboot your computer from the hard disk.

✔ When you are running **MS-DOS 6.0** or higher and you press the F4 or F8 key at the Starting **Windows 95** prompt, running the DIR command may cause strange characters to be displayed if your hard disk is a SCSI drive that requires double buffering and the following line is loading in the CONFIG.SYS (CONFIG.DOS) file:

```
DEVICE=C:\DOS\EMM386.EXE NOEMS X=D800-
DFFF
```

To correct this problem, insert the command

```
doublebuffer=1
```

in your MSDOS.SYS.

✔ After you set up **Windows 95** on a computer with an **EISA** bus, the display adapter may not function, and you may receive the following error:

```
There is a problem with your display
adapter. The hardware settings are in-
correct, or the current settings do not
work with your hardware.
```

and there may be an exclamation point (!) in a yellow circle In Device Manager next to the display adapter, with the following status in the adapter's properties:

```
Device Failure: Try changing the driver
for this device. If that doesn't work,
see your hardware documentation. (Code
27)
```

You may also notice that the display adapter driver is not listed as the correct type. The work-around: use the computer's EISA configuration tool to reconfigure the slot for the correct display adapter type, and then run the Add New Hardware Wizard to redetect the display adapter. To redetect the display adapter:

1. Click the Start button, point to Settings, and then click Control Panel, and double-click the System icon.
2. On the Device Manager tab, click the incorrect display adapter, and then click Remove.
3. When you are prompted to restart your computer, click No, and then click Close.
4. Click the Start button, point to Settings, and then click Control Panel.
5. Double-click the Add New Hardware icon, and then click Next.
6. When you are prompted "Do you want Windows to search for your new hardware?" click Yes, and then click Next.

For information about configuring the slots in your computer, Microsoft suggests you consult your computer documentation or manufacturer.

✔ Microsoft acknowledges that **Windows 95** cannot load a Windows 95 driver over an **OEM** driver of the same name. This means that if you install an original equipment manufacturer (OEM) driver -- such as a printer or display driver -- you cannot later update the OEM driver with the Windows 95 version of the same driver. The work-around: manually extract the Windows 95 version of the driver from the Windows 95 disks or CD-ROM and copy it over the OEM driver of the same name.

✔When you run **Windows 95** Setup from within Windows 95, you may receive the following error:

```
In order to upgrade this version of
Windows, you must run Setup in MS-DOS
mode.  To do this, click Start, click
Shut Down, and choose Restart The Com-
puter In MS-DOS Mode. Then run Setup
from the MS-DOS prompt.
```

The work-around: Exit Setup, restart your computer in MS-DOS mode, and then run Setup again.

✔When installing **Windows 95**, you may receive the following error:

```
Error SU0358
Setup detected one or more MS-DOS-based
programs running on your computer. Close
your MS-DOS programs, and then click OK
to continue. Or, click Cancel to quit
Setup.
```

The work-around: press ALT+TAB to cycle through the running programs and close the MS-DOS-based program.

When you try to play a sound (.WAV) file, you may receive an error such as:

```
Sound Recorder cannot record or play
back because a sound device is not in-
stalled. To install a sound device,
click 'Add New Hardware' in Control
Panel.
```

if there is no

```
drivers=MMSYSTEM.DLL
```

line in the [boot] section of your SYSTEM.INI file.The work-around: add that line.

✔ **Windows 95** may freeze when you start it for a second time after installation if you manually add a SCSI adapter to the system using the Add New Hardware Wizard, AND you incorrectly set the resource settings for that adapter. The work-around: start Windows 95 in safe mode and remove the incorrect SCSI adapter entry.You can safely remove both entries.Then, after you start Windows 95 in normal mode, the detection option from the Add New Hardware Wizard detects the SCSI adapter and sets it up using the correct resources.

✔ If you have a hard drive that requires that device drivers (such as a hardcard driver) load from the CONFIG.SYS file, an interactive boot is not possible with **Windows 95**.The work-around: use a system disk from the previous operating system and boot from the floppy disk drive.

Chapter 4 -- Communications

A 'black art' revealed

So you've got a modem and want to use this Internet thing you keep hearing so much about?

Unfortunately, until now, installing and using a modem and communications software on a PC has been a bit of a "black art." The good news is that with Windows 95 the whole area of communications has become a lot more approachable. Well almost!

Plug and Play technology plus the new Unimodem driver interface for data, fax, and voice modems should, in theory, make light work of installing and configuring your modem in Windows 95.

Theory and practice diverge a bit, however, as owners of Hayes Ultra 1440 modems find when Windows 95 lowers the default speed of the modem. This is not the only instance where comm speeds are slower in Windows 95 than Windows 3.1, as owners of some US Robotics, Intel and Gateway modems will also discover.

As far as your existing communications programs are concerned, most will work individually well enough with Windows 95, though remote access programs such as pcAnywhere (Symantec) and Cross Connect (Smith Micro) have severe problems or are not supported at all.

The main problem is how they work with the rest of your system. You can expect to suffer from port availability conflicts when running both legacy 16-bit or DOS applications and the 32-bit TAPI-aware applets supplied with Windows 95. Since you won't benefit from improvements in the communications architecture until you upgrade your old programs to 32-bit versions, you may be better advised to stick with the Windows 95 supplied software for a while.

This may not be such bad news — Windows 95 comes with a lot as standard, so unless you have specialist requirements, or specifically want upgrades of your favorite programs, you are likely to find all you need right out of the box. For instance, Windows 95 has HyperTerminal, for calling older, text-based bulletin boards and Phone Dialer for dialing voice numbers from your electronic organizer.

If you want to connect to a remote host computer or network you can use Dial-Up Networking (DUN) by installing a pseudo-network component called the Dial-Up Adapter. Due, however, to a last minute change by Microsoft, you must buy the optional Dial-Up Server software in the MS Plus! Pack if you want to configure your computer as the remote host.

Some of the MS Plus! Pack components can be freely downloaded from the Microsoft Network. But you'll need to be a signed up member to do this, so it might well be more economical to shell out for the Plus! Pack.

Bug/Fix Success Rates for Communications

The raw success rate for Windows 95 on Communications related issues is good: better than 65 percent. Despite some sputtering, most people appear to be getting through.

Biggest Communication Problem

In terms of smoke and heat, the biggest communication problem under Windows 95 has undoubtedly been the conflict between the WINSOCK.DLLs used by Windows 95 and Compuserve's Internet dialer.

Biggest Surprise

Lotus cc:Mail chokes on X.400 or VAX messages if the address header is longer than 86 characters.

Direct Cable Connection (DCC) substantially improves on the MS-DOS 6 Interlink utility, and can replace your aging copy of Laplink to connect two computers locally by cable. In addition to file transfer, DCC allows sharing resources such as CD-ROM drives and printers on the host computer.

Unfortunately, Microsoft has not made DCC compatible with Interlink or LapLink, so you must have Windows 95 installed on both PCs. Also, disappointingly, they appear to have been very conservative with transfer speeds, limiting them to about 750 kB/min; so you can expect DCC file transfers to take 2-3 times longer than under LapLink for Windows.

Setting up a direct link to the Internet using the Windows 95 TCP/IP protocol, Dial-Up scripting, an Internet Browser and a DUN connection to a Service Provider such as CompuServe PPP, is supposed to be easy, thanks to the InterNet Setup Wizard in the Plus! Pack. However, unless you are completely at home with the concept of DNS numbers, proxy servers and IP addresses, you are still going to need the helpful services of a tame InterNet expert.

MS Exchange, designed as a universal "in-box" which coordinates fax and electronic messaging from a variety of sources such as local network mail or Internet email via a service provider, has, unfortunately, proved to be very heavy on computer resources. Early users have reported long launch times and unusably slow execution on computers with less than 8MB.

Users trying MS Fax, now integrated as a client of Exchange and quite well featured in its latest incarnation, will be appalled by its operational inefficiency compared with Winfax Pro. Unfortunately, Winfax does not perform faultlessly under Windows 95 either, so until Delrina ships a 32-bit replacement, it seems that sending and receiving electronic faxes will remain problematic.

Finally, at this point you should watch out for software which claims to be Windows 95 compatible but which in reality is only slightly modified Windows 3.1 software. For example, Travelling Software says you should be using the latest 6.0b of LapLink for Windows with Windows 95, but it doesn't support long filenames, so you could end up inadvertently overwriting valuable datafiles.

Of course, Microsoft is guilty of this too. Its new Internet Explorer only works with Windows 95, and thus violates Microsoft's own requirement that all Windows 95 software also be compatible with Microsoft Window NT.

Windows 95 Communication Bug & Fix List

'Hear me talkin' to ya' and other favorites...

¥ Delrina confirms there are known problems with Windows 95, **Adobe Type Manager** and all current versions of Winfax. While ATM 3.x fonts appear to be available, they will not print to the Winfax Driver and will be substituted by TrueType fonts. Currently, there is no solution and the only workarounds are to use TrueType Fonts, revert to Windows 3.1, or use a different fax application. The next release of WinFax will not be subject to this limitation.

✔ If you get an error like:

```
(TCP/IP) Lost Connection
```

while downloading files from **America Online** (the error usually occurs near the 50 percent point), you need to upgrade your America Online software to at least version 2.0a.

Bug & Fix List Legend: The symbol ¥ denotes bugs, incompatibilities and other difficulties. The symbol ✔ denotes problems which have either been fixed, or resolved with some sort of acceptable work-around. Products are listed in alphabetical order.

¥ If you try to run ScanDisk in Windows 95 on an **AT&T** computer, you may receive the following error message:
`ScanDisk cannot check the drive as it is not properly formatted or a utility has locked it, format the hard disk or wait for the utility to finish and re-run ScanDisk.`
This problem can occur if you are running BGMAIL.EXE (a tool that is installed on AT&T computers to provide access to AT&T's proprietary mail services). The work-around: edit the WINSTART.BAT or the AUTOEXEC.BAT file and place a semicolon at the beginning of the Bgmail.exe line to temporarily remark it out. Save and close the file and then restart Windows 95 and run ScanDisk.

¥ ScanDisk conflicts with the TSR installed by **AT&T Mail 2.5** or earlier, preventing it from repairing disk problems. Microsoft suggest contacting AT&T for information about an upgraded version.

✔ There is a conflict with versions of **cc:Mail** prior to 2.1 and Windows 95. With the earlier version, if your path statement in your AUTOEXEC.BAT file is greater than 128 characters, cc:Mail will not run. The current release is 2.21 and will work with Windows 95.

¥ Lotus **cc:Mail 2.0, 2.01, 2.02, 2.03, 2.1, 2.2 for Windows** can't read X.400 or VAX messages if the address header is greater than 86 characters. The message is delivered, but the recipient can't open it.

¥ Using the **Chameleon 4.0** utilities in Windows 95 may cause GPFs because Chameleon 4.0 is incompatible with the Microsoft TCP/IP protocol. The work-around: either remove the Microsoft TCP/IP protocol from the list of installed network components and use the NetManage TCP/IP stack. or — to use Chameleon 4.0 with Windows 95 and keep the Microsoft TCP/IP protocol installed on the system — install the NetManage TCP/IP protocol included with Chameleon and unbind the Microsoft TCP/IP protocol from all installed network clients and services. To unbind the Microsoft TCP/IP protocol, Microsoft advises:

1. Click the Start button on the taskbar.
2. On the Settings menu, click Control Panel, then double-click the Networks icon.
3. In the Network components list, double-click Microsoft TCP/IP or click Properties.
4. Click the Bindings tab.
5. Make sure all check boxes are cleared (not selected), then click OK.

✔ Installing the networking component of Windows 95 will overwrite a crucial file and disable **CompuServe NetLauncher 1.0**, resulting in a

```
Fatal Dialing Error
```

when you attempt to run NetLauncher from the CompuServe Internet Dialer program or WinCim. This file is WINSOCK.DLL, which is in the \WINDOWS subdirectory. If you have not yet loaded Windows 95, copy the WINSOCK.DLL file to your \CSERVE\WINCIM, \CSERVE\MOSAIC, and \CSERVE\CID directories. If you do this, then this version of Winsock will be loaded instead of the Windows 95 version. If you have already installed Windows 95, it should have renamed the pre-existing Winsock as \WINDOWS\WINSOCK.OLD. You will have to copy this file to the above directories, and then rename it WINSOCK.DLL. For more information, GO NETLAUNCHER on CompuServe.

¥ **CompuServe Navigator for Windows 1.1** will run under Windows 95, with one exception. The sessions window will not longer automatically scroll down as results come in. You will have to manually scroll with the scroll bar.

¥ Attachmate Tech Support has confirmed that you will not be able to have the **CrossFax** fax scheduler loaded and also access 32 bit communications in Windows 95 (e.g. dial MS Network or register Win95 online). This is due to an incompatibility with TAPI compliant (32bit) and MAPI compliant (16bit) applications. The fax scheduler can be disabled by removing it from the "Startup" group.

✔ If you are using FutureSoft's **DynaComm Elite 3.44, 3.501** or **3.51** with Quick Start, make the menu font "System" in the Windows 95 Desktop/Appearances properties settings to avoid stall. Users of 3.501 should contact the manufacturer to obtain a new version of TIXWX.DLL that fixes problems going to a Novell SAA Gateway.

¥ **E-Mail Connection 2.03** has trouble accessing CompuServe and MAPI services under Windows 95. Contact the manufacturer (that's ConnectSoft now; no longer Adonis) to obtain a Windows 95-compatible version.

¥ In SofNet **FaxWorks Pro / Voice 3.0e**, when sharing a modem, Win32 applications may not see it as a printer port. The command button to go to the call center from any other application does not work.

¥ At this time **LapLink for Windows 6.x** does not support long file names. Simply moving files between machines is OK, but the long file names will not display during the copy. Problems will occur using the Synchro features when the file names have the first 6 characters in common. Keeping the first 6 characters of the long file names unique will avoid this problem but doing a straight copy is better.

¥ **LapLink Remote Access** is not compatible with Windows 95. Users will need to start Windows 95 in the DOS mode, set up WIN95 to be a dual boot machine, and boot back to Windows 3.x when they need to use LLRA; or upgrade to LapLink for Windows 6.0b, which is fully functional in Windows 95.

✔ If you are unfortunate enough to click the More Information button on the Diagnostics tab when you are viewing the properties for a Microcom **DeskPorte 28.8 Fast EP modem**, you may receive an error like:

```
The modem failed to respond. Make sure
it is properly connected and turned on.
Verify that the interrupt for the port
is properly set.
```

followed by

```
The computer is not receiving a response
from the modem. Check that it is plugged
in, and if necessary, turn it off, and
then turn it back on.
```

The problem is that Windows 95 modem diagnostics do not work correctly with the Microcom DeskPorte 28.8. The work-around: turn the modem off and back on (but don't click the More Information button on the Diagnostics tab).

✔ When using with Dial-Up Networking in **Netscape 1.1** for Windows NT, Microsoft says you may need to add the line

```
DDE Hosed=Yes
```
to the [Main] section of the Netscape INI file.

✔ The "File Send" command in some programs, such as Microsoft **Works 3.0**, Lotus **1-2-3** and Adobe **Pagemaker** may not work reliably to send a fax with **Microsoft Fax** in Windows 95. The work-round: either attach the file to a fax or File Print to the Fax driver from within the program.

¥ Microsoft has designed the Contact Manager in **Schedule+** (now part of **Office 95**) so that names and addresses added there cannot be accessed from within Microsoft Exchange. Until this amazing oversight is corrected, it's probably best to use Exchange for email addresses and Schedule Plus for everything else.

✔ If you install the pen driver that ships with Fractal Design **Painter 1.2**, you may receive the error message:
```
This application's attempt to get access
to COM<x> has failed because the port is
in use by a virtual device.  Press a key
to continue.
```
where <x> specifies a particular communications port. Upgrading to Fractal Design Painter 2.0 and choosing to use the existing pen drivers during Setup corrects this error.

¥ HyperTerminal will not recognize hot insertion of a **PC-Card modem** if the program is already running with a communication session loaded.

¥ When you use Microsoft Fax with a **Practical Peripherals PM144MT II** or **PM14400FXSA fax/modem**, you may not be able to receive faxes. According to

Microsoft, the Practical Peripherals PM144MT II and PM14400FXSA fax/modems require firmware updates to work correctly with Microsoft Fax.

✔ Moving the mouse while downloading files using Datastorm Procomm Plus 2.0 for MS-DOS may cause your computer to freeze. The work-around is to upgrade to at least Procomm Plus 2.01 (files dated 5/91)

¥ When you exit **Qmodem for Windows 95**, the SHUTDOWN.WAV file gets chopped off in mid-wave. Mustang Software acknowledges this, and in the future will be adding a pause in the shutdown sequence, so that the entire .WAV file will be heard.

✔ After installing Windows 95 and restarting your computer, your installed Intel **SatisFAXtion internal fax modem** may not work, and the following error message may appear:

```
Write fault error writing comm<x> when
attempting to access the fax modem from
an MS-DOS prompt.
```

where <x> is the number of the serial port on which the modem is configured. Also, when you try to dial in Hyperterminal, the system may freeze or fail to dial. The work-around: install the real-mode device drivers from the installation disks provided with the Intel SatisFAXtion internal fax modem card.

✔ If you find that Windows 95 cannot gain access to your communication (COM) ports after installing a new modem, the problem may be that you have the communications application **SuperVoice 2.0b** installed on your system. The work-around: open your SYSTEM.INI and change the line that reads:

```
COMM.DRV=RHICOMM.DRV
```

to

```
COMM.DRV=COMM.DRV
```

Save the changes and then restart your system.

✔ If you use the old DOS navigator for Compuserve, **TapCIS**, you may find that Windows 95 Exchange can't find your COM port after you use TapCIS, forcing you to reboot to get Exchange to work. The work-around: Add the line

```
COMxAutoAssign=2
```

(where "x" is the number of your COM port) to the [386Enh] section of SYSTEM.INI and reboot Windows 95.

✔ If you are experiencing what has become affectionately termed the "spiral of death" using a **US Robotics 28.8 Sportster** and Windows 95 (the connection dies after a few minutes, and the only to reactivate the modem is to turn it off and on), you probably need the update BIOS (11/94). It's free and can be ordered by email from US Robotics at 76711.707@compuserve.com.

✔ If you have trouble connecting with your Internet service provider using a **US Robotics 28.8 Sportster** modem, you may need to try a new INIT string. Open Control Panel/Modems/Properties/Connection/Advanced. In the Extra Settings box, type

```
&F&B1&H1&R2&A3&K3X4S56=128S54=96
```

✔ **WinCIM 1.4** has a conflict with Windows 95 which will cause article windows not to print. Other objects (such as email or forum messages) print correctly. According to CIS

WinCIM Technical Support Staff, to correct the problem you need to edit your WIN.INI file and add the following line to the [Compatibility] section `WINCIM=0x4`.

¥ If you have a FAX server (32 bit) waiting for an incoming call, and then **WinCim 1.4** (16 bit) is opened, you may get an error informing you that the port is already in use. The FAX server MUST be turned off in order for WinCim 1.4 to get control.

✔ Microsoft confirms a bug in MS Fax which results in **Windows 95** Cover Pages not appearing in the "Compose a New Fax" dialog box if the archive bit of one or more Cover Page files has been set off (e.g., by a backup utility program). The fix is to restore the archive attribute to the files using the following command at an MS-DOS prompt: `ATTRIB +A C:\Windows\*.CPE`.

¥ It is not possible to receive incoming faxes if a **Windows 95** PC has the Dial-Up Server software installed and active. You can send faxes, but incoming calls will always be answered by Dial Up Networking. Microsoft explains this limitation is due to the Server software being hard coded to answer on the first ring. It is not possible to override this with a modem "AT" command or by editing the registry. At present, the only fix is to disable the server temporarily when incoming faxes are expected.

¥ Microsoft has confirmed that if you uncheck the option to "Use Country Code and Area" in the Dial Up Networking Properties dialog, it actually also deactivates the dialing properties. A Microsoft spokesman says Product Development people are looking at the problem and will fix it in a future release of **Windows 95**.

✔When you use the **Windows 95** DriveSpace compression utility to delete a compressed drive, you may get the following error message

```
Windows cannot perform this operation
because the enhanced mode disk compres-
sion driver could not be loaded. You may
need to run setup again to install addi-
tional disk components. DRVSPACE 545
```

To correct this problem, extract the file DRVSPACX.VXD from the original Windows 95 disks or CD-ROM. To extract the file, open a DOS window and type

```
extract /l <drive
letter>:\windows\system\iosubsys
<drive letter>:\win95_11.cab
drvspace.vxd
```

where <drive letter> indicates the letter designating the drive containing the floppy disk or CD-ROM. Then restart your system.

✔When you change modem-specific settings in the Modem Properties dialog box in **Windows 95**'s Microsoft Fax, the fax transport may not use the new settings. For example, the fax transport does not use a new Speaker Volume or Answer After <n> Rings setting. To make sure the new settings are used, restart the application that will use them. For example, you must restart Microsoft Exchange after you change modem-specific settings in Microsoft Fax.

✔ If HyperTerminal, the Microsoft Network, or another TAPI-enabled application do not dial, the problem is probably that a pre-Windows 95 service provider appears in the TELEPHON.INI and precedes the **Windows 95** Universal Modem Driver (UNIMDM). To work around this problem:

1. Open the TELEPHON.INI file that is in your Windows directory with a text editor.
2. The Providers section may appear as follows:

```
[Providers]
NumProviders=2
NextProviderID=3
ProviderID0=1
ProviderFilename0=ATSP.TSP
ProviderID1=2
ProviderFilename1=UNIMDM.TSP
```

The following changes should be made:

```
[Providers]
NumProviders=2
NextProviderID=3
ProviderID1=1
ProviderFileName1=ATSP.TSP
ProviderID0=2
```

✔You are unable to connect to a **Windows 95** Dial-Up Networking server when running a Windows for Workgroups Remote Access Service (RAS) client, Windows NT 3.1 RAS client, or Windows 95 Dial-Up Networking client. This problem can occur if the Dial-Up Networking server you are connecting to is a Windows 95 computer set up as an NWSERVER and the client is using the RAS drivers instead of the Point-to-Point protocol (PPP) drivers. The work-around: use the Windows 95 Dial-Up Networking client in PPP mode or the Windows NT 3.5 RNA client in PPP mode.

✔ HyperTerminal, Dial-Up Networking, Phone Dialer, and the Microsoft Network are **Windows 95** applications that place the number "1" at the beginning of a phone number to be dialed if the number has a different area code than your default area code. Some countries (Canada, for example) have telephone numbers that are in different area codes but that are not long distance calls. To manually change this in HyperTerminal

1. Click the Start button, point to Programs, and then click Accessories.
2. Click HyperTerminal Connections.
3. Double-click the icon that was created when you made a new HyperTerminal connection.
4. In the Dial dialog box, click the Modify button beside the phone number.
5. Click the Phone Number tab, then change the area code to match your local area code.
6. Type the phone number you want to dial, including the area code, in the Phone Number box.

To enable Dial-Up Networking to dial a telephone number with a different area code as a local number:

1. Click the Start button, point to Programs, and then click Accessories.
2. Click Dial-Up Networking.
3. Double-click the icon that was created when you made a new Dial-Up Networking connection.
4. On the Connect To dialog box, remove the "1" from the phone number field.

To enable Phone Dialer to dial a telephone number with a different area code as a local number:

1. Click the Start button, point to Programs, and then click Accessories.
2. Click Phone Dialer.

3. On the Tools menu, click Dialing Properties, then click New.
4. Enter a new location. For example, TEST.
5. For the TEST location, enter the area code for the number you want to dial, then click OK. For example, 555.
6. Type the number you want to dial in the Number To Dial field. To enable The Microsoft Network to dial a telephone number with a different area code as a local number:
1. On the Sign In screen for The Microsoft Network, click the Settings button.
2. Click the Access Numbers button.
3. In both the Primary and Backup boxes, delete "+1" from the beginning of the access number.
4. Click OK.

¥ Believe it or not, **Windows 95**'s HyperTerminal can't delete characters that are already on your screen. Selecting text and pressing the Delete key does notclear the screen. Other than exiting HyperTerminal and restarting it, no workaround is available.

¥ If you are using a video board with one of the older video chip sets by **S3**, and you have your modem on COM4 in **Windows 95**, the modem lights may flash when you move the mouse or when there is any disk or network activity. The work-around: either reassign the modem to another comm port, or use a Windows version 3.1x S3 video driver. Note, however, that when you use a **Windows 3.1**x video driver in Windows 95 you lose some of the Windows 95 functionality (such as mouse cursors, mouse trails, and fallback video support). Microsoft says this problem does not occur with the 964/984, trio/64/32, or 866/868/968 chip sets and will not occur with any newer chip sets released by S3.

✔You may receive the following error message while you are running **Windows 95** Exchange:

```
Error 171 could not access schedule
information if a virus-checking program
is run on the postoffice and is protect-
ing the MAILDATA share. The virus-check-
ing program can prevent the MS-DOS ADMIN
program from manipulating the message
files it needs.
```

The work-around: disable the network virus-checking program, or set it to not protect the MAILDATA share.

✔ If you're suffering from communications problems after an upgrade to **Windows 95**, you should comment out or remove any line in the [386Enh] section of your SYSTEM.INI that starts with COM (e.g., COMxFIFO, COMxBUFFER etc).These remnants can cause 16550 Uart chips to lockup.

✔When making a Dial-Up Connection under **Windows 95**, your User ID and Password is supposed to be passed automatically to the $PASSWORD variable in a Dial-Up Script, but this may not happen if you're dialing from Exchange.The work-round: code the password into the Dial-Up Script so that it doesn't have to be entered manually each logon.

✔ If you are having difficulty connecting two PCs together via Direct Cable Connection in **Windows 95**, check that you haven't set both computers with the same name.To connect successfully each PC must have unique names.

✔ If you set your COM port to IRQ2, you must select IRQ9 in **Windows 95**.The real IRQ2 handles the cascade to the second interrupt controller and the old IRQ2 signals come in on IRQ9, according to James McDaniel of ZiffNet. So, your hardware should be set to IRQ2, and your software to IRQ9.

¥ If you arrange the icons in **Windows 95** Dial-Up Networking folder, you'll find the next time you open the folder, the icons are rearranged back the way they were originally. There is no work-around at the present.

✔ When you try to start **Windows 95** Internet Explorer, you may receive the following error message:
`Error: Out of memory. Close some programs, and then try again.`
This happens when virtual memory has been turned off. The work-around: enable virtual memory. Here's how:
1. Click the Start button, point to Settings, and then click Control Panel.
2. Double-click the System icon.
3. On the Performance tab, click Virtual Memory.
4. Click the "Let Windows manage my virtual memory settings (recommended)" option. Or, if you must use your own virtual memory settings, allow as much space as possible for the maximum size.
5. Click OK.

¥ If you drag an Internet shortcut with a number sign (#) in its filename to the **Internet Explorer's** client area, you receive the following error:
'file:C:\internet\Favorites\<filename>' could not be found. The attempt to open 'file:C:\internet\Favorites\<filename>' failed or was canceled.

even though the shortcut will work in **Windows 95**. There is no work-around at this point.

¥ Although the **Windows 95** Microsoft Fax Cover Page Editor has an Undo feature that lets you undo up to five tasks, you can undo only one task in a text box.

✔ When you are sending a fax with **Windows 95 Fax**, you may receive the error message:

```
WordPad caused a General Protection
Fault in WPSUNI.DRV
```

if there is an older version of FAXCODEC.DLL in your Windows folder or directory. The work-around: find and remove the FAXCODEC.DLL file from the Windows folder. The correct Windows 95 version of the FAXCODEC.DLL file should be located in the WINDOWS\SYSTEM folder.

✔ The **FaxDirect** program that ships with the DOS versions of WordPerfect 5.1 and WordPerfect 6.x will not work with **Windows 95** if you load FaxDirect in the Windows 95 AUTOEXEC.BAT. Novell recommends that you start WordPerfect and load FaxDirect from a batch file after Windows 95 has started. It is also important to select both Prevent MS-DOS-Based Programs from detecting Windows and Suggest MS-DOS mode as necessary.

✔ If WordPerfect 5.1 or 6.x for DOS is run while in **Windows 95** and you try to access either the fax send or receive logs of **FaxDirect**, your computer may freeze. The work-around: shut down Windows 95 and restart the computer in Single Application mode. Then load the fax drivers and run WordPerfect from the DOS prompt.

¥ If your modem needs to dial a number, such as "9," in order to access an outside telephone line, it can be entered into a field in Dialing Properties for any TAPI aware program to use. However, this number is ignored by the **Windows 95 Phone Dialer** and also programs, such as Schedule+, which are configured to use it as a dialing applet. The only work-around may be to dial the number manually.

✔ The properties for the PCMCIA modem in your computer may show the wrong port name, even though the modem functions correctly under **Windows 95**. If two PCMCIA devices each have a "PortName=COMx" setting in the registry, the "port-friendly" name for the original device is used for both devices. For example, if you install a GPS PCMCIA card, then remove the card and install a PCMCIA modem, the Port field for the modem may display the friendly name for the GPS card.

✔ Microsoft, in its infinite wisdom, has made it very hard for some people to remove the Microsoft Network from their computers. For instance, if you try to get rid of MSN by clearing The Microsoft Network check box on the **Windows 95** Setup tab, you may receive an error such as:

```
There is not enough disk space for all
the selected components. Click OK and
then clear one or more of the selected
components.
```

The happens if there is less than 2 megs of free disk space on your hard drive (even though you'd think that deleting files wouldn't require disk space). The work-around: close all running programs, which will shrink your swap file. If this doesn't do it, try removing all the programs in the Startup folder and disable the "load=" and "run=" lines in your WIN.INI file.

✔ In **Windows 95** Exchange, if you get the error

```
Can't launch form
```

when composing or reading a message, then your forms file may be corrupt. To correct this problem, exit Exchange, delete Frmcache.dat from \WINDOWS\FORMS, copy FRMCACHE.BAK to FRMCACHE.DAT, and restart the program.

¥ The **Microsoft Mail 3.x** extensions, **WinRules** and **Conference+** are incompatible with **Windows 95** Exchange. Most problem extensions are automatically removed by Exchange but it may be necessary to disable others manually by putting a semicolon in front of the extension's load line in MSMAIL.INI. Contact the extension vendor for more information.

✔ Forms created with the **Microsoft Electronic Forms Designer** and saved in the .MSG file format do not open correctly in **Windows 95** Exchange. To avoid this problem, transfer the .MSG file from the file system to the Inbox.

¥ In **Windows 95** Exchange, if you enter over 35 characters in the "Name to show on cover page" field in the Fax address book, the overflow characters spill into and overwrite the telephone number field.

¥ If you are downloading a file with **Windows 95** HyperTerminal, you should make sure you have plenty of hard disk space to receive the file because, believe it or not, the program cannot detect when a disk becoems full during the download.

✔ If you already have a TAPI service provider running on your computer under **Windows 3.1**, you will find that HyperTerminal does not work properly when you upgrade to **Windows 95**. To fix this you should use the Telephony icon in Control Panel (if you can find it: see below) to remove and then reinstall the TAPI service provider from within Windows 95.

✔ Some users have reported finding a strange file In the **Windows 95** System directory (usually C:\WINDOWS\SYSTEM) called TELEPHON.CP$. This seems to be a misnamed Control Panel Applet. If you rename it to TELEPHON.CPL then a fresh icon (labeled "Telephony") appears in the Control Panel. Microsoft did this to avoid confusing users, according to Toby Nixon, Program Manager, Windows Telephony.

✔ In **Microsoft Fax** in **Windows 95**, if you want to include a message on your cover page, you must ensure that the cover page template contains the "note" field. If this is absent, your message will actually appear on the second page of the fax.

✔ Microsoft reports (with stunning precision) that if you change a setting in **Microsoft Fax** while **Windows 95** Exchange is running, your alterations will "probably" not take effect until you log off, exit from Exchange and then restart it.

✔ In **Microsoft Fax** in **Windows 95**, performance is best for short notes with the message placed on the cover page, but if you are using the "New Message" form from Exchange you can't put the message there. Instead, to do this you must use the "Send Fax" wizard (Compose / New Fax).

✔When you use the fax configuration properties sheet to browse to a cover page in **Microsoft Fax** in **Windows 95**, a link (.LNK) to this cover page is created in your Windows directory. If you already have a cover page (.CPE) in your Windows directory with the same name, this name will appear in the cover pages list twice, but you can select only one of them. It is recommended that you delete one of the files by using Windows Explorer.

✔ If you get the following error message when trying to Create a New Message in MS Exchange:

```
Object not found Error in Microsoft
Windows Messaging Systems Forms Registry
13085 8004010F
```

this is because damage has occurred to the Windows 95 registry. Maurice Jeter of WUGNET recommends removing Exchange via Control Panel/Add/Remove Programs, then adding it back in. To keep your previous address book and information store, answer Yes when Exchange asks if you've used Exchange before. When encountering this error, however, it may be necessary to run **Windows 95** setup directly from CDROM/Disk and choose to verify the current installation copying only damaged or missing files. This appears to actually copy *all* files; but it will keep your previous Windows 95 configuration intact.

✔ If you use **Windows 95** to send a fax to a **Windows for Workgroups 3.11** At Work Fax user, and the message includes multiple recipients on the CC: list, the only addresses that will be visible on the fax user's message are the fax addresses. However, all messages will be sent correctly.

✔ When you upgrade **Windows for Workgroups** with Remote Access Service (RAS) support installed, programs that use the WINSOCK.DLL file may no longer function properly. The work-around: replace the **Windows 95** WINSOCK.DLL file with the older version of the file, or obtain an updated version of the third-party program that will function correctly with the Windows 95 Winsock.dll file.

✔ There is a known problem when using the "Attachments" function of **Winfax Pro** under Win95, which results in the error message

```
This program has performed an illegal
function and will be closed down.
```

Delrina says the problem occurs in some versions (earlier than July 28 1994) and is related to the toolbar button. they suggests using the Menu Selections instead of the button. The latest maintenance release (dated May 26, 1995) is available by downloading the textfile WNET4.TXT (Lib 12) and following the instructions.

✔ Attempting to install **WinFax Pro 4.0** under Win95 will give the message:

```
You should temporarily disable this
desktop before installing WinFax
```

followed by instructions on how to do this. These instructions are not relevant to Win95 and can safely be ignored according to Frank Flood of Delrina.

¥ Brad Johnston of Delrina has confirmed that because the DDE macro language has changed in the Windows 95 versions of MS Office products, macros written to integrate products such as **Excel 5** and **Word 6** with **Winfax**

Pro will no longer function correctly with the 32-bit **Microsoft Office 95** products.

✔ Many users of **Winfax Pro 4** have reported problems faxing from the new **Microsoft Office 95** applications, **Word 7** and **Excel 7**. These include Word 7 hanging when trying to fax a document to the fax printer driver; giving error messages such as
`Windows Cannot Print Due To A Problem With The Current Printer Setup`
(possibly related to the use of Cover Pages). Delrina says things are improved by sending and receiving faxes in the foreground and also recommends turning off the "Background Printing Option" in Word 7. Some users have found an improvement by reinstalling Winfax Pro 4 after installing Windows 95 and MS Office 95 in that order.

✔ Many printing problems using **WinFaxPro 4** under Windows 95 can be solved by adding the WinFax directory to your path statement in your AUTOEXEC.BAT file.

✔ If you are having problems in printing when using **WinFax Pro 4** in conjunction with Word 95, disable background printing in Word with Tools, Print, Options.

¥ Delrina Technical Support has stated that **WinFax Pro for Networks 4** does not work with Windows 95, and they will not support it.

¥ If cover pages in **WinFaxPro 4** contain **Adobe Type Manager** fonts, they will not fax correctly, and they often will not display correctly either. Cover pages without ATM fonts will work fine.

✔ If you install the **Word 7** "Address Book" option from **Microsoft Office 95** and haven't got MS Exchange installed on your computer; you may get an error message `Unrecoverable Error - MAPISVC.INF is missing` (among other cryptic dialogs) when you try and insert an address from your Schedule+ Contact List. If however, you have installed **Netscape 1.2** (32 bit version, beta 6 or later) then a MAPISVC.INF will be present and Win95 will attempt to run the InBox Setup Wizard, even though you may not have the MS Exchange installed. The workaround, such as it is, for both the Word 7 Address Book and Netscape problems (which are of course related), is to install MS Exchange.

Chapter 5 -- Windows 95 Games

Welcome to Gamers' Hell!

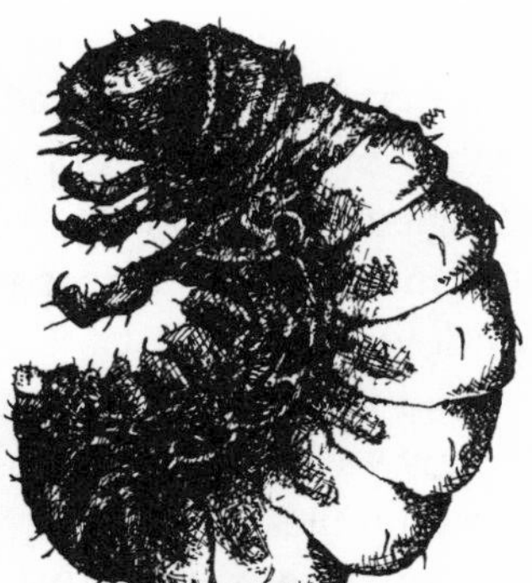

More than exploding stones or a talking dog, gamers who venture into the new Windows 95 world are going to need an old fashioned knowledge of expanded memory, device drivers, and boot disks.

Sound familiar? In an almost Calvinist twist, people who want to play games in Windows 95 are forced to suffer more than people who just want to count beans. The reason is not deific pique, however, but rather the "legacy" of DOS.

To achieve the graphics and animation needed, DOS game developers have long pushed the limits of the C:\ prompt, crafting custom programming solutions which often required every ounce of muscle MS-DOS could muster.

Windows 95 does wonders for developers of new games, but it doesn't do that much for players of old DOS games. Many of these games were a pain to properly configure in DOS, and they remain a pain. Judging the glass half full, Computer Gaming World declared DOS game setup under Windows 95 "certainly no worse than configuring them for DOS."

The first new Windows 95 games like Pitfall Harry's Mayan Adventure are beginning to appear on the shelves, but so far few gamers have been weaned from their old DOS standbys.

Basically, there are three choices for installing DOS games under Windows 95. If you've been living right, you can simply create an icon for the game, and run it (see list). Windows offers a choice of full screen or windowed-mode, but most players will opt for full screen for performance reasons.

If that doesn't work, and it won't for a significant number of popular DOS games, you'll have to run the game in Single Application Mode, which is to say in exclusive MS-DOS mode, which forces you to reboot to get back into Windows 95 (see list).

And finally, if that won't work, you'll have to boot from a floppy with your old pre-Windows 95 version of DOS and setup files.

If you find your beloved game falls into the great Single Application Mode heap, here's what you do. Go Explorer, open the directory which contains the game and find the .EXE file that runs the game. Highlight it, right click your mouse, and choose Properties. Select the Program tab at the top of the box, and then the Advanced button, and finally click "MS-DOS mode."

Now things get a little dicey. Each game can have its own AUTOEXEC.BAT and CONFIG.SYS file containing

Bug/Fix Success Rates for Games

The raw success rate for legacy DOS games running under Windows 95 is not especially good. If you want to play games, expect to suffer a little.

Biggest Game Problem

The biggest problem for demanding old DOS games is making enough system resources available to them so that they can do their thing (sound familiar?).

Biggest Surprise

Doom, Heretic, X-COM: UFO Defense, and Day of the Tentacle are among the games that can be run from inside Windows 95 with no tweaking at all.

drivers for your CD-ROM drive, mouse, etc. Chances are, you are going to have to manually add this information from your old pre-Windows 95 AUTOEXEC.BAT and CONFIG.SYS files.

To do so, you "Specify a new MS-DOS configuration," and copy the lines from your old setup files into the appropriate windows. It's best to start with just the drivers you think you'll need, and then add more little by little if necessary.

Some games require not only substantial amounts of conventional memory — as much as 610K for "Aces of the Pacific," for instance — but also a megabyte or more of expanded memory. For this, you'll need a memory manager like Netroom or QEMM.

One caveat: be certain that there is no blank line at the end of the new AUTOEXEC.BAT file that you create for your game's Single Applications Mode setup. When you've got the AUTOEXEC.BAT and CONFIG.SYS files the way you want, click "Use current MS-DOS configuration."

Now if you're lucky, when you double-click on the game's icon, your machine will reboot and up will come your DOS game.

Are we having fun?

Windows 95 Games Bug & Fix List

Wherein Daedalus Encounters Doom, Flight Commander, Descent and much more...

¥ The **3 Balloons: Alphabet, Numbers & Shapes** educational game by SWeDe will cause GPFs if you try to switch to another task while a QuickTime movie is playing.

¥ If you switch to another task from Microsoft's **500 Nations**, you may encounter weirdness in the desktop wallpaper or in other programs that require the color palette.

¥ A number of compatibility problems have surfaced in Virgin Games's **7th Guest**. Some versions of PAS 16 require IRQ 5 and DMA 3 or else the MS-DOS Prompt will stall. If you store the game on **ATI Mach 64**, horizontal

---

Bug & Fix List Legend: The symbol ¥ denotes bugs, incompatibilities and other difficulties. The symbol ✔ denotes problems which have either been fixed, or resolved with some sort of acceptable work-around. Products are listed in alphabetical order.

lines will appear on the screen, and the game won't run at all on Compaq QVision.

✔ The Windows-based installer may not work correctly with Sierra Online's **Aces -- The Complete Collector's Edition.** The workaround: use the MS-DOS-based installer instead.

✔ **Aces of the Deep** by Dynamix needs to run in MS-DOS Mode.

✔ **Are You Afraid of the Dark 1.0** from Viacom requires MS-DOS Mode.

✔ If you find that Berkeley System's popular **After Dark** screen saver interrupts your game sessions — even when it is turned off — go into the Advanced settings for the screen saver and disable "allow screen saver in DOS sessions."

✔ A click of the mouse in **Alien Legacy 1.0** from Sierra Online can cause a 10-20 second pause if sound was enabled for SoundBlaster Pro on IRQ 10. A lower IRQ setting will solve this problem.

✔ Alistair and the **Alien Invasion** may not install correctly under Windows 95. Windows 95 Help automatically explains how to report the appropriate Windows version number to the setup program.

✔ Display problems show up during the installation of Interplay's **Alone in the Dark 2.0**, but the program, but don't be alarmed, the program will install correctly.

✔ **Amazon Guardians** of Eden by Access Software will not quit when you press CTRL+Q because of changes in the Windows operating system. Instead, you must press ALT+SPACE and then click Close.

¥ **Anglo-Saxons** from Cambrix is a Windows 2.x program and is not supported under Windows 95.

✔ If you are plagued with GPFs during installation of Avtec's **Animal Tales,** do not despair. The application will nevertheless install and run correctly.

✔ When you try to play certain movie clips in **The Animals,** you may receive the error message:

```
Stack Overflow
```

The work-around: upgrade to The Animals 2.0.

¥ In Software Toolworks **The Animals 1.0**, GPFs may occur when some movies are played.

¥ Animotion **CDMaster**'s volume control doesn't work with some sound cards.

¥ In Corbis Publishing's **A Passion for Art**, GPFs may occur when ejecting the CD and then exiting the program.

¥ In addition to some minor taskbar irregularities, Corbis's **A Passion for Art** has palette errors when the Network dialog box is displayed.

✔ **Archon Ultra** from Free Fall Associates requires MS-DOS Mode.

✔ **Arctic Baron** from ReadySoft requires MS-DOS Mode.

✔ **Around the World in 80 Days** by Electronic Arts will not run in Windows 95 on all systems. Try it in MS-DOS Mode.

¥ **Astronomical Explorations** from EMME runs all right, but problems show up when you repaint the screen after switching to another task. It's best to avoid this, according to Microsoft.

✔ **Battle Chess 4000 1.0** from Interplay will work better if you start it from the Start menu instead of a command prompt.

¥ The **Battle Chess Enhanced CD-ROM** from Interplay won't run on Compaq QVision with VESA using the Windows 95 display driver.

✔ **Battledrome 1.0** from Dynamix / Sierra requires MS-DOS Mode.

✔ Because **Betrayal at Krondor** requires a great deal of memory, Microsoft advises: "Try using the Make Boot Disk option from INSTALL."

✔ **Betrayal At Krondor** requires a lot of EMS memory, and for that reason many people have found that they must run it in Windows 95's Single Application Mode, AND they must load an extended memory manager like Netroom or QEMM in Krondor's Single Application Mode setup.

✔ Depending on your video adapter, you may have problems with the video playback in **Beyond Planet Earth** from Discovery Communications. The workaround: add

```
vidc.cvid=iccvid.drv
```

in the [drivers] section of SYSTEM.INI.

✔ **Bioforge 1.01** from Origin requires MS-DOS Mode.

✔ **Bloodnet** from Microprose will not run with Pro Audio Spectrum 16 sound card unless DMA = 7. Two workarounds: use SoundBlaster emulation or run in MS-DOS Mode.

✔ **Brett Hull Hockey 95** from Accolade requires MS-DOS Mode.

¥ **Bring the World to Your Senses** from Sampler CD will not install or run on Windows 95 . It needs Windows 3.0.

✔ **OsoSoft Bubba95 1.2 for Windows** requires 640x480 resolution for proper display.

✔ **Busytown** from NovaTrade may require MS-DOS Mode on some systems.

¥ **Solitaire** and **WinMine** don't work on CD Mania 1.0 by Aristosoft because they rely on the **Windows 3.1** versions of these programs. The icon change does not affect Windows Explorer icons.

✔ **Chessmaster 3000** from The Software Toolworks may require MS-DOS Mode on some systems. Also, check to see that digital sound is turned off (which should be by default) or the computer may stall after sound effects.

✔ **Children's Writing and Publishing Center 1.5** from The Learning Company may require MS-DOS Mode on some systems.

✔ **Chuck Yeager's Advanced Flight Simulator** from Electronic Arts can install under Windows 95 but it must run in MS-DOS Mode.

✔ Viacom's **Club Dead 1.0** requires MS-DOS Mode.

¥ Older versions of Microprose **Colonization Windows CD** do not run under Windows 95, stalling shortly after the game starts. Microprose has released a patch.

¥ If you have the **Colorforms Computer Fun Set** from Gryphon Software that's labeled "4 Seasons of Fun," everything's fine. But with other versions Windows 95 fails when the user fills a region with paint.

✔ Virgin Interactive Entertainment's **Creature Shock** will be (blessedly?) silent on SoundBlaster AWE32 unless it is run in MS-DOS Mode.

¥ **Critical Path** from Media Vision may not work correctly with some ATI video adapters.

¥ Domain's **Crystal Walls 1.0 for Windows** has some troubles. New installations under Windows 95, will hide the Crystal Walls wallpaper beneath the desktop. Upgrades from earlier Windows, show the wallpaper but not the animation. Windows 95 Help includes information for obtaining an update from the manufacturer.

✔ **Curse Of The Catacombs 1.0** from FroggMan requires MS-DOS Mode plus a bit of skill. You must manually configure the program properties in Windows 95 to run in MS-DOS Mode.

✔ SCI's **Cyberwar** may have sound problems with some configurations. If you have an ESS ES688 sound card, choose SoundBlaster within the game. If problems occur, use MS-DOS Mode.

¥ In Mechadeus **Daedalus Encounter 1.0**, GPFs or system stalls can occur soon after starting this program. Contact Machadeus for an updated version.

✔ The demo of Lucas Arts' **Dark Forces 1.0** requires MS-DOS Mode. The sound card detection must run twice during installation to detect AWE 32.

✔ **Darkseed 1.5** from Cyberdreams, Inc. requires MS-DOS Mode.

✔ Although **Day of the Tentacle** runs under Windows 95, it may not run if you establish a Windows 95 shortcut to this game's "shell" program. The work-around: run it from TENTACLE.EXE.

¥ **Death Gate** by Legend Entertainment should be run in MS-DOS Mode, and even then you may have difficulties if you computer has an ESS 688 or Aztech WA sound card.

✔ To get **Descent** to run in Windows 95, you may need to reinstall the program and run setup from Windows 95 for proper sound. It may be slower than under DOS though, so you may want to run it in Single Application mode.

✔ This isn't a problem, just a minor delay. When installing Interplay's **Descent** with SoundBlaster AWE 32 sound cards, the program seems to stall while testing music. Be patient; it's just slow.

¥ The hotkeys for Delrin'a **Dilbert Screen Saver 1.0** don't work under Windows 95.

✔ **Dino Park Tycoon 1.0** requires MS-DOS Mode to use sound.

¥ **Dinosaur Adventure 3.0** will not produce digitized speech on SoundBlaster-type sound cards.

✔ In order to restore the **Disney Collection Screen Saver** after it has been minimized, first right-click on the taskbar button. Then choose the control panel from the popup menu.

✔ FroggMan's **Dognapped** requires MS-DOS Mode.

✔ When running **Doom**, many users have found it helpful (even necessary sometimes) to make a bootdisk with the appropiate AUTOEXEC.BAT and CONFIG.SYS files and use that to start your computer. Others, however, have been able to run it under Windows 95 as long as they kept the Doom window maximized.

✔ If you press CTRL+ALT+DELETE and quit **Doom 2**, when you restart Doom 2, you may find that the sound effects are no longer present although the music may still play. The work-around: don't use CTRL+ALT+DELETE to quit the Doom 2 program.

¥ Neither **Doom 1.6** nor **Doom 2** from ID Software will run in an MS-DOS Prompt on systems that are paging through MS-DOS. You will need MS-DOS Mode to meet your doom. Also, Doom 2 won't run using **Gravis Ultrasound Max** under Windows 95.

✔ When you run the game **Dracula Unleashed** by Viacom in a Windows 95 MS-DOS session, your computer may freeze. According to Microsoft: "Windows 95 should automatically run Dracula Unleashed in MS-DOS mode. However, you may have to delete any Dracula.pif files first. If Dracula Unleashed still does not run properly, set the game's properties manually." To do so:

1. In My Computer, right click the Dracula Unleashed icon, and then click Properties.
2. In the Dracula Unleashed Properties dialog box, click the Program, and then the Advanced button.
3. Confirm the MS-DOS mode box is checked.
4. Select the Use Current MS-DOS Configuration button, and click OK.

For the game to run properly, you also may have to add a sound card, a mouse, or CD-ROM support.

✔ You can run Viacom's **Dracula Unleashed CD** on Windows 95 as long as you use a SET BLASTER variable and MS-DOS Mode.

✔ Merit Software's **Dragon's Lair** must be run in a full-screen MS-DOS Prompt.

✔ **Dragon's Lair CD-ROM** from ReadySoft needs to run in MS-DOS Mode directly from the CD-ROM. Do not run the setup program that copies Dragon's Lair from the CD-ROM to the hard disk.

¥ Users get display problems when using QVision display cards with **Dr. T's Sing-A-Long Around the World**.

✔ **Dune II** from Virgin Games may require the factory-default settings for sound cards. This problem is not specific to Windows 95, but worth mentioning.

✔ Software Heaven's **Dungeon Master 1.0** may require MS-DOS Mode on some systems.

✔ **EarthSiege** and **EarthSiege 1.0** from Dynamix / Sierra both require MS-DOS Mode.

✔ **Eight Ball Deluxe 2**.0 from Amtex may require MS-DOS Mode on some systems.

¥ Gameteks' **Hell - A Cyberpunk Thriller** may have no sound during introduction if your machine has an ESS688 sound card installed.

¥ Some video clips in Microsoft **Encarta '93** will not play under Windows 95. The only work-around is to upgrade.

¥ When you look up a word in the Microsoft **Encarta 1995** Dictionary or Thesaurus, you may get the error:

`DICT caused a General Protection Fault in module REDLLWIN.DLL.`
or
`This program has performed an illegal operation and will be shut down. If the problem persists, contact the program vendor.`
To recover: exit Windows, turn your computer off, then on again. At this point, Encarta can be restarted. There is no work-around to prevent these system freezes at present, however.

¥ Setting the time delay for PC Dynamics' **Energizer Bunny 1.0** requires keyboard commands. You won't be able to use the mouse under Windows 95. Also note (sigh), the minimized icon for the program is not animated.

✔ **ESPN - Winning Hoops with Coach K** from Intellimedia Sports reports an error during installation, but it's OK to ignore it. The program will load and run with no problems.

✔ The CD-Rom of **F-15 Strike Eagle III** from Microprose requires EMS memory. Windows 95 Help provides information.

✔ When you try to start the Spectrum Holobyte game **Falcon 3.0** in an MS-DOS window in Windows 95, you may receive an error message like
`Cannot Open File`
even when the FALCON3 directory is in your PATH statement. Microsoft says, "To start Falcon 3.0, you must be in the FALCON3 directory. When you create a shortcut for Falcon 3, the working directory must be FALCON3."

¥ **Falcon AT** from Spectrum Holobyte is not designed for 486-based PCs and may run too fast to play. Users of MS-DOS 6.22 will recognize this behavior.

✔ The third edition of Multimedia's **Family Doctor** displays an error message when the program starts. Just ignore it.

¥ In Gametek **Family Feud**, a memory leak occurs with 8-bit sound cards, so the system eventually runs out of memory under Windows 95. Restarting Windows 95 will correct the system resources.

✔ **Jasmine Multimedia - Famous Places** has trouble copying INDEO.DRV, but Windows 95 Help automatically provides a solution.

¥ **Fantasy Pinball** is one of the few games we've encountered that seems to demand that you reboot in "good old" MS-DOS. When set up as a Single Application Mode program, the system may reboot without ever running the program.

¥ **Far Side Screen Saver Collection 1.0** from Delrina may have difficulty if you run MS DOS-based graphics-mode programs that accept mouse input, accoridng to Microsoft.

✔ **Fields of Glory 1.15** from Spectrum Holobyte may require MS-DOS Mode on some configurations.

✔ Electronic Arts's **FIFA International Soccer** requires MS-DOS Mode.

¥ **Firefighter!** from Simon & Schuster Interactive will corrupt the Windows 95 palette. You may also get problems with sound/video matchup when using with Compaq QVision.

✔ When you try to start **Fleet Defender F14 Tomcat 1.0** by MicroProse, you may receive the error:

```
F14 This program has performed an ille-
gal operation and will be terminated.
Quit all programs, and then restart your
computer.
```

The work-around: increase expanded memory as much as possible:

1. Use the right mouse button to click the Fleet Defender icon, and then click Properties.
2. Click the Memory tab.
3. If the Expanded Memory box contains the message "The computer is not configured for expanded memory in MS-DOS sessions," click the Details button and set the Expanded (EMS) Memory setting to Auto.
4. Click OK until the dialog box closes.

✔ If you try to start Microprose **Fleet Defender F14** in Windows 95 when another program is already using MIDI, you may receive an error like:

```
This program has performed an illegal
operation and will be terminated. Quit
all programs, and then restart your
computer.
```

The work-around: make sure that no other programs are using MIDI.

✔ **Flight of the Intruder** from Spectrum Holobyte requires MS-DOS Mode. But first you must manually configure the program properties in Windows 95 for MS-DOS.

¥ In Spectrum Holobyte **Flight Simulator Toolkit CD**, a GPF can occur after selecting the world editor icon and then clicking in the editing region.

¥ The icon may be displayed incorrectly in the Control Panel for the **Flintstones Screen Saver Collection 1.0** from Delrina.

¥ Davidson's **Flying Colors** may fail under Windows 95 after you use several tool icons. Contact the manufacturer for a possible update.

¥ According to Microsoft, you'll need to get a patch from Franz Inc to run **Franz Allegro CL 2.0 for Windows** under Windows 95.

✔ **Freakin' Funky Fuzzballs 1.03** by Sir-Tech requires MS-DOS Mode. You should manually configure the program properties in Windows 95 to run in MS-DOS Mode.

✔ If you play **Freddy Pharkas** in an MS-DOS session in Windows 95 on a computer with Microsoft Windows Sound System-compatible hardware, the game may not produce any sound. The work-around: reconfigure the Windows Sound System-compatible device to use IRQ 7 and DMA 1, or create a shortcut to the game that specifies MS-DOS mode.

✔ **French Pronunciation Tutor 3.0** by HyperGlot may show a minor display corruption when switching tasks, but it works.

✔ **Front Page Sports Baseball '94** by Sierra Online requires MS-DOS Mode.

✔ **Front Page Sports Football Pro '95** by Sierra Online requires MS-DOS Mode.

✔ **Front Page Sports: Football Pro!** by Dynamix works with DMA channel. Otherwise the game will stall or the sound won't work.

✔ Lucas Afts **Full Throttle 1.00 CD** requires that you run the sound card detection twice during setup to enable sound support for AWE32.

✔ **Full Throttle** may not run under Windows 95 unless you go to the "Advanced Program Settings" under the Program Menu, and change its properties sheet so that it does not detect Windows.

¥ **FX Fighter** from GTE Entertainment / Argonaut sometimes shows faults in the extender.

✔ **Gabriel Knight for DOS** by Sierra Online requires MS-DOS Mode.

¥ **Gadget Invention**, Travel & Adventure by Synergy has a minor problem. The background screen blacks out when Save To Network dialog box is open.

¥ Slash Corporation **Gambler's Paradise Casino Pack I** installation program may fail.

¥ **George Shrinks** by MediaStation does more than shrink. It disappears from the task bar if you switch away and then switch back.

✔ **Goblins 2** from Sierra Online requires MS-DOS Mode.

✔ **Great Naval Battles - 1939-1942** from Strategic Simulations requires that you manually configure the program properties in Windows 95 to run in MS-DOS Mode. The program itself can run in a full-screen MS-DOS Prompt from Windows 95. You must also use Vinstall to detect correct VESA driver.

¥ Grolier acknowledges that the **Grolier Multimedia Encyclopedia 1995** has trouble printing text to certain printers. The company is working on a fix. If you have trouble, contact Grolier.

✔ **Aegis - Guardian of the Fleet** from Software Sorcery must run in MS-DOS mode.

¥ The screen may shift up on some Compaq QVision displays in **Accolade Hardball 4**.

✔ **Harpoon II** by 360 Pacific requires MS-DOS Mode.

✔ After you install **TSoft Head Coach Football for Windows** under Windows 95, you may get the following error:

```
SU installed correctly...but could not
add group to Program Manager
```

although the game runs properly.

¥ **Heart: 20 Years of Rock & Roll** by Compton's New Media will show the wrong script font unless you have upgraded to Windows 95 from Windows 3.1.

¥ **Heart: 20 Years of Rock & Roll** by Compton's New Media has problems with Windows 95's sound scheme (not the best news for a music program), according to Microsoft.

✔ **Helicopter Simulator** from Sierra Online requires MS-DOS Mode.

¥ If you use an **ATI** video board with 256 color wallpaper to play Time Warner **Hell Cab 1.0**, the screen may go black.

¥ On some computers you get problems such as page faults when quitting or when running the introduction to **Raven's Heretic 1.0**.

¥ Impressions' **High Seas Trader** is plagued by GPFs when running in an MS-DOS Prompt with Aztech Nova 16, SoundBlaster 2.0 and PAS 16 SoundBlaster-emulation soundcards.

✔ You will may have problems with the CD-ROM version of **3D Home Architect** by Broderbund if you are on a network printer. The workaround: make sure a printer port is mapped to the network path instead of a UNC name. Redrawing captions may also present difficulties under Windows 95.

¥ **Horde** by Crystal Dynamics requires MS-DOS Mode.

¥ **Horde** by Crystal Dynamics may not run on Aztech Nova 16 or Aztech WA 16.

✔ Gametek's **Humans** requires MS-DOS Mode.

✔ Sierra Online's **Inca** requires MS-DOS Mode for both disk and CD versions.

✔ **Indy Car Racing** from Papyrus requires MS-DOS Mode.

¥ The **Infopedia Add-on: Galaxy of Stars** Multimedia Tour from FutureVision runs poorly on low-memory computers. Maybe a shorter name would help?

¥ Installing **Interactive Calculus Windows CD** from D.C. Heath on a remote hard drive causes the system to stall, so don't do that.

✔ **Ishar 3** from ReadySoft must be installed and run in MS-DOS Mode.

¥ **Island of Dr. Brain 1.1** by Sierra Online will stall on Aztech sound cards.

✔ **Isle of the Dead** from Merit Software requires MS-DOS Mode. The user must first manually configure the program properties in Windows 95 to run in MS-DOS Mode.

✔ Although you may be able to install **Jagged Alliance** under Windows 95, some users report that it randomly reboots their machines. It is probably preferable to run the game from a DOS boot disk.

¥ Paramount Interactive **Jump Raven** does not run under Windows 95.

✔ **Jutland** by Software Sorcery requires MS-DOS Mode.

¥ Davidson's **Kid Cad 1.1 Windows CD** Show Me mode requires the Windows 3.1 Macro Recorder. This is not available in a new Windows 95, although it is available when Windows 95 is installed as an upgrade.

✔ If the volume control slider in **Kid-Fun** by Mindplay doesn't work correctly, use the Windows 95 Sound Volume control.

✔ In Broderbund **Kid Pix 2 for Windows**, GPFs may occur when using print setup with UNC-named printers. You can avoid them by capturing the printer port. Check the Windows 95 Help file for instructions.

✔ **King's Quest III** from Sierra Online requires MS-DOS Mode.

✔ **King's Quest VII** from Sierra Online installs only on drive C.

¥ Knowledge Garden **KnowledgePro 2.11 for Windows** cannot run under Windows 95.

✔ Sales Curve's **Lawnmower Man** requires MS-DOS Mode.

¥ Input using the Spanish keyboard layout for HyperGlot **Learn to Speak Spanish** 5.0 does not work properly.

✔ **Legend of Kyrandia - Book 3: Malcolm's Revenge** by Westwood Studios requires that you modify the manufacturer's PIF manually, as described in the release notes.

¥ **Legend of Kyrandia - Book 3: Malcolm's Revenge** by Westwood Studios runs without sound if using Aztech Nova 16 WSS emulation. (Could this be a blessing?)

✔ Psygnosis **Lemmings, Lemmings Chronicles 3.0** and **Lemmings II** all require MS-DOS Mode.

✔ Access **Links 386** disk and CD require MS-DOS Mode.

✔ Access **Links 386** disk and CD will show the screen shifted up on Compaq QVision displays.

¥ Microsoft acknowledges that "the animations do not play correctly" in **The Lion King 1.0**. The work-around: upgrade to The Lion King version 1.1.

✔ **The Lion King 1.1 CD-ROM** produces sputtering sound with an ESS488 sound card when running under Windows 95. The work-around: use your CD-ROM drive's real-mode drivers instead of the Windows 95 protected-mode drivers.

✔ According to Microsoft, the error you get during Berkeley Systems **Looney Tunes Animated Screen Saver** can be safely ignored, and the program will still work fine.

✔ State Impressions' **Lords of the Realm** should be started from Windows Explorer in order to get better performance.

✔ Sierra Online's **Lost in Time** may need to be run in MS-DOS Mode on some computers.

✔ You may need to add
`"device=c:\windows\command\ansi.sys`
to CONFIG.SYS for Activision's **Lost Treasures of Infocom** to display properly.

¥ **Lower Your Score with Tom Kite Shot Making** from Intellimedia Sports gets weird when used with Video 7 cards.

¥ When you start the compact disc version of **Secret Weapons of the Luftwaffe** and select Historical Overview, you may get an error like:

```
Incorrect DOS version
REDIRECT EXEC FAILED — UPSHOT.EXE
CD="D:\LUCAS\SWPTL\HF;  ...
```

Microsoft advises that you run the game only in MS-DOS mode.

¥ Cyberflix **Lunicus** won't run correctly under Windows 95. This is a Win32S-based program and it replaces some DLLs in the SYSTEM directory. The installation program displays a missing-file error. Contact the manufacturer for information.

¥ Hyperbole Studios **Madness of Roland** may crash just after starting.

¥ **Magic Carpet** runs in Windows 95, but there have been complaints that is extremely slow.

¥ In Bullfrog Productions **Magic Carpet 1.0**, GPFs may occur during introduction.

✔ When you run **Magic School Bus Explores the Solar System**, you may receive the error:
`Problem loading or finding files. Please run Magic School Bus Setup again.`
Unfortunately, reinstalling the program may not fix the problem. This problem can occur if you have The PC Speaker driver installed. If so, you must remove it under Control Panel / Multimedia / Audio.

✔ When you run the **Magic School Bus - Solar System** demonstration on the Windows 95 CD-ROM as part of Microsoft Exposition, the screen may turn black after the music begins if you are using a color palette with more than 256 colors. The work-around: change the color palette to 16 or 256 colors. To do so:
1. Use the right mouse button to click the desktop, then click Properties on the menu that appears.
2. Click the Settings tab.
3. Change the Color Palette setting to 16 or 256 colors, and click OK.

✔ Access Software's **Martian Memorandum** will not quit using CTRL+Q. Instead, press ALT+SPACE and then click Close.

¥ **Math Blaster Mystery: The Great Brain Robbery: Pre-Algebra** from Davidson will not run properly with Gravis Ultra Sound MAX.

✔ Davidson **Math Blaster Episode 2: Secret of the Lost City 1.0** needs some special handling when installing the CD version, CTL3DV2.DLL must be copied to the Windows SYSTEM directory for this program to run.

✔ Software Toolworks **Mavis Beacon Teaches Typing 1.25** requires MS-DOS Mode, as do the other versions earlier than 3.0.

¥ **Mean 18** by Accolade does not run under Windows 95.

✔ **MechWarrior 2** will run under Windows 95, but there have been reports of problems with crashes. It is probably best to run the game in Single Application Mode.

¥ Software Toolworks **MegaRace** will stall after playing for a while on Aztech WA 16 and Aztech Nova 16. For all sound cards, using SoundBlaster rather than SoundBlaster Pro drivers results in better performance.

✔ **Word Perfect Mental Math 2.01** a requires MS-DOS Mode to run without aggravating stalls caused by problems with the real-mode sound driver.

✔ **Mickey's 123's** from Disney requires MS-DOS Mode.

¥ In Disney's **Mickey and Crew Screen Saver**, problems may occur with Windows 95 wallpaper.

¥ Disney's **Mickey and Crew Screen Saver** incorrectly requests a floppy disk when installed using Add/Remove Programs option.

¥ Lifestyle Software **Micro Kitchen Companion Multimedia**'s shopping wizard can cause GPFs.

✔ If your sound card isn't listed in the installation instructions for **MIG-29 1.01.1** by Spectrum Holobyte, choose "PC Speaker" or else obtain an update from manufacturer.

✔ Sierra Online's **Mixed-up Mother Goose** requires MS-DOS Mode.

¥ **Monty Python's Complete Waste of Time** by 7th Level does not waste time so completely under Windows 95, do to weirdness with some of the "Pythonizer" components.

¥ Some of the Pythonizer components in **Monty Python's Flying Circus Desktop Pythonizer** by 7th Level may not operate properly.

¥ Hi Tech's **Mortal Kombat** stalls on Aztech Nova 16.

✔ **Mortal Kombat 2** from Acclaim Entertainment requires MS-DOS Mode.

¥ The Close button on Broderbund's **Myst 1.0** is displayed incorrectly. Bad news. It locks the CD drive even after exiting the game. **Myst 1.0, 1.02** and **1.03** all work fine.

✔ Papyrus Design Group's **NASCAR Racing** is best run in Windows 95's Single Application Mode on most systems. If you want the game to load in high resolution mode, you need to add the -h parameter to the command line, e.g.,

```
NASCAR -H
```

according to game guru James Wilson.

✔ National Geographic **Mammals CD-ROM** requires MS-DOS Mode. The user must manually configure the program properties in Windows 95 to run in MS-DOS Mode.

¥ Any printing from National Geographic **Mammals CD-ROM** requires a non-PostScript printer.

✔ National Geographic CD-ROM **Picture Atlas of the World** requires MS-DOS Mode. You must manually configure the program properties in Windows 95 to run in MS-DOS Mode.

¥ We hope you like Asymetrix's **Natural States Screen Saver** because it cannot be minimized after maximizing.

✔ Electronic Arts' **U.S. Navy Fighters** requires MS-DOS Mode.

¥ Electronic Arts' **U.S. Navy Fighters** will not run on computers that have more than 16 MB (the same as under MS-DOS 6.x). Contact the manufacturer to obtain a patch that fixes this problem.

✔ Electronic Arts **NBA Live '95** requires MS-DOS Mode. Also, you must have SET BLASTER in the AUTOEXEC.BAT file.

✔ Epic Megagames' **One Must Fall** requires MS-DOS Mode. You must also remove the PIF file provided with the game, so that Windows 95 can correctly start MS-DOS Mode when this program runs.

¥ In **Warcraft - Orcs & Humans** by Blizzard Entertainment, GPFs can occur when running in Single Application Mode. This program fails on Aztech Nova 16, SoundBlaster 2.0 and PAS 16 SoundBlaster-emulation when running under Windows 95.

✔ **Oregon Trail Deluxe** from MECC requires MS-DOS Mode for sound.

✔ On Sierra Online's **Outpost 1.1**, the left-click won't restore this program from the task bar but the right-click will.

✔ **1942 - The Pacific Air War** by Microprose needs to be run in MS-DOS Mode.

✔ **1942 Gold - The Pacific Air War** by Microprose uses a Windows-based setup program. When you click the shortcut created, it exits Windows and tries to run C:\DOS\COMMAND.COM before starting the game, which results in the error message: Incorrect DOS version. The word-around: copy the Windows 95 COMMAND.COM to the DOS directory.

✔ Origin's **Pacific Strike** uses a VCPI-protected mode and requires MS-DOS Mode.

✔ **Pagemaster** from Turner Interactive sometimes has problems when you first start the program on some CD drives. Usually it will work if you cancel and rerun.

✔ **Panzer General** is best run in Windows 95's Single Application Mode on most systems.

¥ If you're using a SoundBlaster clone, **PC Karaoke Classics (from Vol 1) 4.0** from Sirius Publishing may have problems recognizing it. The fix is to use a true SoundBlaster card.

✔ In Time Warner Interactive's **Peter and the Wolf**, under Windows 95, you cannot install the some drivers that the program requests each time the program starts. If you answer No to the request, the program will run correctly.

✔ In Electronic Arts **PGA Tour Golf 486**, GPFs can occur with certain hardware. Should be run in MS-DOS Mode to avoid problems.

✔ **Pinball 2000 2.0** from Expert Software may require MS-DOS Mode on some systems.

✔ **Pinball** players using a non-U.S. keyboard will find that the right flipper key does not work because it does not have a default setting. International gamers should therefore set an alternative key for the flipper using the Player Controls on the Options Menu.

✔ **Pinball Arcade CD-ROM** from 21st Century Entertainment requires MS-DOS Mode.

✔ **Pinball Fantasies** from 21st Century Entertainment requires MS-DOS Mode.

¥ **Pink Panther Screen Saver** Entertainment by Asymetrix overwrites title bar controls. Now that's entertainment.

¥ System sounds for **Pink Panther Screen Saver** Entertainment by Asymetrix may not be listed in the Sounds Control Panel.

¥ When you try to run **Beyond Planet Earth** in Windows 95, you may receive the error message:

```
SBP Caused a General Protection Fault in
SBPUSA.EXE
```

if you are using the High Color (16 bit) or True Color (24 bit) color palette. The (unacceptable) work-around: set your video card to use the 256 Color or 16 Color palette.

✔ **Police Quest IV Open Season** from Sierra Online must use SoundBlaster and not Soundblaster Pro. Windows 95 Help automatically provides information.

✔ Activision **PowerHits BattleTech 1.01** requires MS-DOS Mode. You need to manually configure the program properties in Windows 95 to run in MS-DOS Mode.

✔ Activision **PowerHits Movies** requires MS-DOS Mode. You must manually configure the program properties in Windows 95 to run in MS-DOS Mode and ensure that the working directory is set properly.

¥ **Privateer**, from Origin, uses a memory manager that conflicts with Windows 95. The only way to run it is to shut down to DOS and reboot with a floppy prepared to run Origin (and/or other demanding DOS games).

✔ Origin's **Privateer** requires MS-DOS Mode, 579K conventional memory, and 2.5 MB EMS.

✔ Front Page **Sports Pro Football 95** is best run in Windows 95's Single Application Mode on many systems. You may also find you need to load an extended memory manager like **Netroom** or **QEMM** in Pro Football 95's Single Application Mode setup.

✔ **Putt-Putt Joins the Parade (DOS)** from Humongous Entertainment may need a PIF setting to ensure the correct Windows version information. It also requires MS-DOS Mode, and the user must manually configure the program properties in Windows 95 to run in MS-DOS Mode.

¥ In Media Vision **Quantum Gate**, random GPFs can occur during play.

¥ In Media Vision **Quantum Gate**, the cursor display is incorrect, and the Set Volume and MIDI controls are nonfunctional.

✔ Gametek's **Quarantine** requires MS-DOS Mode.

✔ **Quest for Glory IV** from Sierra Online needs to run with SoundBlaster rather than SoundBlaster Pro.

✔ Interplay's **Rags to Riches** runs only in a full-screen MS-DOS Prompt.

✔ **Random House Unabridged Electronic Dictionary** may create invalid hotkeys. To create a hotkey that works, use the Windows 95 shell.

✔ In **WordPerfect Read With Me 1 & 2 for Windows CD** under Windows 95, printing from Coloring Box might lock up the system. The workaround: print from Word Traveler.

✔ **Realms of Arkania - Blade of Destiny 3.0** from Sir-Tech requires MS-DOS Mode with 600K conventional memory.

✔ **Rebel Assault 1.4** from Lucas Arts requires MS-DOS Mode if running REBEL.EXE, but you might be able to run REBEL2.BAT in an MS-DOS Prompt. Help automatically provides information for improving performance on 80386 processors.

✔ **Rebel Assault 1.4** from Lucas Arts has no sound with PAS 16 unless you use an 8-bit DMA channel. Windows 95 Help automatically provides information for improving performance on 80386 processors.

¥ **Red Storm Rising** from Microprose may display an error code with Cirrus Logic display adapter.

✔ **Relentless Twinsen's Adventure** from Electronic Arts requires MS-DOS Mode.

✔ Strategic Simulations **Renegade Battle For Jacobs Star 1.0** might not have sound on PAS 16 (darn). It's better to configure the game to use SoundBlaster emulation.

✔ Installation of Activision's **Return to Zork 1.2** may cause blue-screen error messages under Windows 95; According to Microsoft, these errors can be safely ignored.

✔ The display in Tadpole Productions' **Rick Ribbit Adventures in Early Learning** may have problems if run in anything but 640x480 mode.

✔ **Rick Ribbit in Ark Noodle's Math Challenge** on disk and CD may both have problems running in anything but 640x480 mode. Windows 95 Help automatically provides steps for changing the resolution.

✔ **Rise of the Robots** by Time Warner Interactive requires MS-DOS Mode.

¥ **Rise of the Triad** may run fine under Windows 95, but there have been a few complaints that after you press ESC to get to the main menu to exit, all you get is a blank screen. If you encounter this problem you might want to run the game in Single Application Mode.

✔ **Robinson's Requim** from ReadySoft requires MS-DOS Mode.

¥ **Rocky and Bullwinkle Screen Saver** by Asymetrix will overwrite title bar controls. Also, systems sounds are not listed in the Sounds Control Panel.

¥ In Maxis **Rome**, GPFs can occur on some systems after selecting Quit and Save. You still can play the game though.

✔ **Rules of Engagement 2** from Impressions needs to run in a full-screen MS-DOS Prompt.

✔ Lucas Arts' **Sam N Max Hit the Road** must be installed in MS-DOS Mode. Once it's loaded it can run in an MS-DOS Command Prompt.

✔ **Science Adventure II** from Knowledge Adventure requires MS-DOS Mode. You need to manually configure the program properties in Windows 95 to run in MS-DOS Mode.

¥ **WizardWorks Screen Saver 1992** must run in full-screen mode in an MS-DOS Prompt or else the system will crash when you invoke the program.

¥ After you quit playing Lucas Arts' **Secret of Monkey Island 1.0** the CD music keeps playing. Hope you like it.

✔ **Serf City** by Strategic Simulations must run in full-screen mode in an MS-DOS Prompt.

✔ **Ultima VII - Serpent Isle** and **Serpent Isle Part Two** by Origin require MS-DOS Mode.

✔ Origin's **Shadowcaster** needs to run in MS-DOS Mode if your computer doesn't have a math coprocessor.

✔ **Sherlock Holmes Consulting Detective 1.0** from Icom requires MS-DOS Mode. You need to manually configure the program properties in Windows 95 to run in MS-DOS Mode.

✔ **SimLife** by Maxis needs MS-DOS Mode to run on 486-based PCs. It also may have to be installed under MS-DOS Mode.

✔ Infocom's **Simon The Sorceror** requires MS-DOS Mode with 512K conventional memory. You will need to manually configure the program properties in Windows 95 to run in MS-DOS Mode.

¥ On some computers, Berkeley Systems' **Simpson's Screen Saver** refuses to mute its sound on four modules.

¥ For some configurations, the taskbar loses its Always On Top property in Berkeley System's **Simpson's Screen Saver**.

✔ In Digital Pictures **Slam City with Scottie Pippen**, GPFs can occur when this program is run the first time, but it works after restarting the computer and configuring the game to use the proper sound card.

✔ You must run Cambrix **Small Blue Planet - The Cities Below** in 256-color mode to avoid GPFs that occur in 16-color mode.

¥ Tune 1000 **Soft Karaoke 2.0 for Windows** cannot run under Windows 95.

¥ Sound may not work correctly in the **Southern Living Cookbook** from Lifestyle Software Group if you are using SoundBlaster 16 and 4MB of memory.

¥ For the **Space Quest Collector's Edition** from Sierra Online a dialog box appears in front of the window for the Inside Space Quest utility so the user can hear, but not see, the video play.

¥ According to Microsoft, **Power Spanish** by Bayware is incompatible with Windows 95.

✔ Accolade's **Speed Racer** requires MS-DOS Mode.

✔ **Starship Game** from Merit Software requires MS-DOS Mode, with 580KB conventional memory and careful configuration of sound.

✔ You may have problems copying some animation components in **Star Trek Interactive Technical Manual** from Simon & Schuster Interactive. Windows 95 Help automatically provides information.

✔ Spectrum Holobyte's **Star Trek: The Next Generation - A Final Unity** requires MS-DOS Mode. You will need to manually configure the program properties in Windows 95 to run in MS-DOS Mode.

✔ To use the **After Dark** control panel on Berkeley Systems' **Star Trek: The Screen Saver** when it is minimized, right-click the icon in the taskbar and then select Control Panel from the popup menu.

✔ In **Storybook Weaver Deluxe** from MECC, the installation program may prompt the user to switch to a small font, but the steps provided won't work for Windows 95. Use the Display option in Control Panel to change the fonts.

✔ **Strike Commander** from Origin requires MS-DOS Mode.

¥ The Learning Company's **Student Writing Center 1.0** may have trouble printing to HP printers.

✔ **Super Street Fighter 2** Turbo from Gametek requires MS-DOS Mode.

¥ GPFs can occur in SWeDe **Scavenger Hunt Adventure** Series:Africa if a QuickTime movie is playing when switching from this program's window to a 32-bit program.

✔ **Syndicate** from Electronic Arts requires MS-DOS Mode.

¥ **System Shock** from Origin will cause GPFs if you run it in an MS-DOS Prompt with Aztech Nova 16, SoundBlaster 2.0, or PAS 16 SoundBlaster-emulation sound cards.

✔ **Sytos Plus 1.42 for MS-DOS** from Sytron requires MS-DOS Mode.

✔ **Terminal Velocity** may experience system lockups when run on the Windows 95 desktop. The work-around: run it in Single Application Mode.

¥ In Electronic Arts **Theme Park**, GPFs can occur while switching between the introduction and the game, or when quitting the game.

✔ **Thinkin' Things Collection 2 v 1.0** from Edmark requires a full-screen MS-DOS Prompt. Run TTW2.EXE to start the game.

¥ When running under Windows 95, **Tony La Russa Baseball III** fails on Aztech Nova 16, SoundBlaster 2.0, and PAS 16 SoundBlaster-emulation. Start this program from Windows Explorer in order to get better performance.

¥ **Science for Kids Adventures with Oslo, "Tools and Gadgets,"** can cause GPFs when printing on a PostScript printer.

¥ Older versions of **The Twilight Zone Screen Saver** by Sound Source Interactive may cause GPFs when the screen saver starts. Contact the manufacturer for updated supporting files.

✔ X-Com's **UFO Defense** and **Terror of the Deep** both run under Windows 95, but it's best to set them up with the Screen Options set to "full screen." Otherwise, you will see flashes of the Windows 95 desktop when the program switches executables, as when changing from tactical to strategic view.

✔ **Ultimate Football** by Microprose requires MS-DOS Mode.

¥ **Ultima VII: The Black Gate** (Top Ten Pak) from Electronic Arts will not run on Pentium hardware.

✔ **Ultima VIII: Pagan** requires MS-DOS Mode.

✔ **Ultrabots** (Top Ten Pak) from Electronic Arts requires MS-DOS Mode. You will have to manually configure the program properties in Windows 95 to run in MS-DOS Mode.

✔ **Under a Killing Moon** by Access Software requires MS-DOS Mode.

Chapter 6 -- Windows 95 Publishing

If this is Waterloo, who is Wellington and who is Napoleon?

Like Waterloo in the summer of 1815, it's clear that there is going to be a major battle in the area of PC publication software, meaning word processor, page layout, graphic and electronic publishing programs.

If Windows 95 is to going to attack the Apple Macintosh in its two remaining strongholds, it must make a showing here. This means lots of new releases, and yes dear reader, it means lots of software bugs too.

The beleaguered Mac forces have dug in on the high ground, but the wave of new Windows 95 software has begun its charge. Already we have CorelDraw 6, PageMaker 6, Word 95, and WordPro — with many more programs scheduled to make their appearance in the months ahead.

Numbers are crucial to the Windows 95 strategy, for Mac/OS 7.5 for the PowerPC may still be a superior high-end publishing platform. Of course, this could also be said of the dedicated, room-sized computers that ruled commercial publishing a decade ago. The bones of these dinosaurs testify to the fact that the high-end may be where publishing platforms go to die.

Now Windows 95 is trying to do to the Mac what the Mac did to Compugraphics and company. To succeed, it must essentially isolate and overwhelm the enemy. Windows 3.x has already prepared the ground by defeating the Mac (and PostScript as well) in the low- and middle-end publishing markets (if you can have a "middle-end"). The tide is clearly running in Windows' favor, but the Mac forces grimly fight on.

Which brings us back to bugs. While Mac devotees continue to prattle about "ease of use," this weapon has largely been blunted by the new Windows 95 user interface. In addition, the Mac has its own problems with bugs and stability. The well-publicized problems of Word 6 for the Mac are only part of it. In one of the few extensive comparative real world OS tests that have been conducted, The Computer Paper found that that Mac/OS was actually less stable than Windows 95 was *in beta*.

But what about the final version of Windows 95 as released to the public, and the publishing software that runs under it? How stable are these programs? How many holes do they have in their functionality, and how much aggravation are they likely to cause their users?

In raw terms, the ratio of fixes to bugs is not particularly good among the publishing software issues raised in this Windows 95 list. Altogether, these publishing programs have a 52 percent success rate; that is to say there are acceptable fixes or work-arounds for 52 percent of the

Bug/Fix Success Rates for Publishing

The raw bug/fix success rate for publishing software running under Windows 95 is not especially good. So far, in fact, it's worse than both Windows 3.x and the Mac over the last year.

Biggest Publishing Problem

Incompletely implemented features are probably the biggest single problem in this group at present.

Biggest Surprise (Not)

CorelDraw 6 (and its allies) have contributed the largest number of problems to this list. If Corel is true to form, it will now work harder than any other vendor to fix them.

problems listed here. This is worse than the average BugNet found for Windows 3.x programs over the last year. It is also worse than the average BugNet found for Macintosh software over the past year, which tallied a 63 percent success rate.

Looking at the product breakdown within the publishing category, it will probably not surprise BugNet readers to see that CorelDraw (and its allies) have provided by far and away the largest number of entries. Corel has a history of releasing particularly buggy products, but it also works especially hard to fix bugs. This is why Corel also has historically scored high on BugNet's Fix/Bug Ratio Chart.

So far, however, Corel's efforts to fix the problems have not been too evident. The company did issue a bug fix less than two weeks after CorelDraw 6 went gold in August, but since then the bugs have been piling up like the dead in front of Wellington's lines.

So as the din of battle rises, the outcome is still undecided. Windows 95 continues to hurl its forces forward, while Apple fights on, awaiting the software equivalent of Blücher's Prussians (Big Blue?) to rescue it.

Windows 95 Publishing Bug & Fix List

Acrobat, CorelDraw, PageMaker,PhotoShop, Word, WordPro, WordPerfect and much more...

✔ Two-up or four-up printing (such as one would use in a brochure) does not work from Adobe **Acrobat Exchange 2.01** with the standard PostScript printer driver installed by Windows 95. The work-around is to revert to Adobe Postscript driver 3.01 or later.

✔ If you change the 3D Objects color in the Display Properties dialog under Appearances, the activated buttons on Adobe **Acrobat Reader 2.1**'s toolbar may get strange. Adobe advises leaving the color settings alone.

✔ If you upgrape to Adobe **Acrobat Exchange 2.0** on a system where Acrobat 1.0 was previously installed (but not completely removed), you may get an error message like:
`Adobe Type Manager`

Bug & Fix List Legend: The symbol ¥ denotes bugs, incompatibilities and other difficulties. The symbol ✔ denotes problems which have either been fixed, or resolved with some sort of acceptable work-around. Products are listed in alphabetical order.

`Old Multiple Master fonts found. Please install new ones.`

The work-around: edit your ATM.INI file to remove references to the old files. Remove all the lines (probably four) which start

```
AdobeSansXMM=
AdobeSerifMM=
```

But DON'T TOUCH the similar

```
AdobeSanMM=
AdobeSerMM=
```

✔ If after installing Adobe Acrobat you find that the **Acrobat PDFWriter** icon in the Printers folder is unavailable, you may need to add the following line to the [Ports] section of the file:

```
DISK:=
```

then save the WIN.INI file and close it, and restart Windows 95.

¥ If you use **Adobe Type Manger 3.0** or **3.01** under Windows 95, you may experience slow printing in PCL mode.

✔ After you install **Adobe Type Manager** into the Windows\Fonts folder, you may receive an

`Invalid Fonts Directory`

error message when you start the ATM Control Panel (ATMCNTRL.EXE), and no fonts may be displayed. The work-around: create a new folder for the ATM fonts and then move the ATM fonts from the Windows\Fonts folder to the new folder. Edit the ATM.INI file in the Windows folder and change the path for the ATM fonts to reflect the new folder.

✔ Double-clicking the Fonts icon in Control Panel does not display **Adobe Type Manager** (ATM) PostScript Type 1 fonts that are installed on your system. You can manually add the fonts to the WIN.INI file, which will cause them to be displayed, but they still cannot be opened (or viewed). To view the installed ATM fonts, run the ATM Control Panel application(ATMCNTRL.EXE) included with Adobe Type Manager.

✔ If you try to print a document on a PostScript printer and you have more than 590 **Adobe Type Manager** (ATM) fonts installed, you may receive a GPF. The work-around: reduce the number of ATM fonts installed.

✔ If you receive the following message when you try to start the **Ami Pro** QuickStart Tutorial in Windows 95:

```
QuickStart Tutorial will not run unless
the AMI Pro window is maximized and the
Border Width is set to 3 in Control
Panel.
```

You need to change the Active Window Border to 1:

1. Use the right (secondary) mouse button to click the desktop.
2. Click Properties.
3. Click the Appearance tab.
4. In the Item box, click Active Windows Border.
5. Change the setting in the Size box to 1.
6. Click Apply Now to accept the new setting, then click OK.

✔ If envelope printing in **Ami Pro 3.1** is giving you problems in Windows 95, here are some suggestions from Lotus Technical Support. First, reinstall AmiPro under Windows 95. This should have created a new AMIPRO2.INI file in the

Windows 95 directory. You need to go back to the old Windows directory, find the old version of AMIPRO2.INI, and copy the EnvUser section, and only this section, to the new version of AMIPRO2.INI.

¥ If you are trying to get by with some really old software, you may run into problems. **Ami Pro 1.2** will not work with Windows 95. Users will have to upgrade to **Ami Pro 3.1** or **WordPro 96**.

¥ EPS images printed with the 2-up option or the 4-up option from **Ami Pro** running under Windows 95 do not print correctly. The work-around: avoid this procedure.

✔ In **Ami Pro, Freelance, Harvard Graphics** and **PageMaker 5**, the Help button may overlap the Close button on the far-right side of the title bar. Microsoft advises using another way to close the application, such as ALT+F4.

¥ English users reports that **AutoCAD release 12**, which ran successfully under the preview version of Windows 95 (in MSDOS mode), will not run at all under the release version, but gives a

`Pharlap extender error`

indicating a memory manager conflict.

✔ If you click on an option on the menu bar in **Microsoft Bookshelf '94**, it may not select the correct option, or the menu bar may become difficult to read. The work-around is to select Bookshelf 94's Normal Menus. To do this:

1. Press the ALT key on your keyboard, then press the letter "T."

2. Click Options.
3. Click the Normal Menus check box to enable this option.

¥ Corel gurus like David Satz on Compuserve report that when running **CorelDraw 4**, they are unable to save files with color bitmap headers. The work-around is to save files with a monchrome bitmap header or no bitmap header at all.

¥ According to Corel, the Equalize filter does not work with **CorelDraw 5 D1, E2 and F2**.

✔ Several TSRs (including the WinCIM spell checker) have been shown to conflict with **CorelDraw 6**'s Layer Manager roll up and cause immediae GPFs. Simply disabling them makes the problem go away, according to the legendary Jose Camara. Check your WIN.INI for

```
LOAD=
```

entries, and disable these utilities.

✔ Saving from **CorelDraw 6** in version CorelDraw 5 format can generate a corrupt file the SECOND TIME you save it. The work-around: After opening the file saved by CD6 in CD5, bring up the styles roll-up and load a new *.CDT style sheet. Saving the file in CD5 format won't corrupt it now. But what if you've already screwed up the file? José Camara has a solution for that too: "If you didn't see this before and already have work lost in an unreadable file, use a binary editor like **XTree** or **Norton DE**, look for the string 'stlt' and replace it with four binary zeroes. After opening, replace the style sheet."

¥ **Corel PhotoPaint 6** won't open Pro-Photo CDs (6144 x 4096 size).

¥ Paragraph text from **CorelDraw 5** files, when opened in CorelDraw 6, changes aspect, and sometimes the last line scrolls off. The work-around: use CorelDraw 5.

¥ In **Corel PhotoPaint 6,** if you open new image (360 x 504, 24 bit), apply a 3D rotation of -70H -43V, with Best Fit selected, and then click on preview, you may get the error:
`PICOR60: error in filter op.`
The work-around: as with the 45 degree line bug in CorelDraw 5, the trick here is to use a slightly different angle ("Only a few combinations give the problem," notes José Camara), or simply don't use preview.

¥ If you create a RGB image in **Corel PhotoPaint 6**, fill it with blue, and then go Effects / Color Adjust / Equalize, you will get a bad preview with garbage in the top two lines. Worse yet, the equalize histogram is calculated on the garbage portion, too. There is no work-around at present.

✔ Effects/Color Adjust/Equalize doesn't work for separate color channels in **Corel PhotoPaint 6**. If you open a RGB image, use Effects/Color Adjust/Equalize, select "red" instead of all channels, and then Preview the image you may see that the changes affect all channels, not just red. The work-around suggested by José Camara: separate to R,G,B. Apply filters individually, merge back to RGB.

¥ Some TIF Preview types in EPS images exported from **CorelDraw 6** can't be viewed in other applications. The work-around: use black-and-white or 8-bit greyscale preview in EPS exports.

✔ Similarly, WMF Preview in EPS images exported from **CorelDraw 6** can't be viewed in other applications like **PageMaker 5**. All you'll see is a box; no visible preview, except in some Corel 6 applications. The work-around, courtesy of José Camara: "The EPS export filter evidently uses whatever setting is current for the WMF export filter when it makes the WMF preview; before doing WMF/EPS exports, export a file, any file, as WMF and clear the Placeable header checkbox in the export dialog box. Quit Draw to make sure the change is written to the INI file. When you start Draw again and export EPS with WMF preview, the Placeable header will no longer be included in the WMF, meaning it'll work in PageMaker et al."

¥ Slanted guidelines may not be recognized in the **CorelDraw 6** Guidelines dialog box, making it impossible to delete them.

✔ In **CorelDraw 6**, if you set drawing scale to 1:200, fountain fill steps will be shown multiplied by 200, so a 16 step fountain fill will be listed as 3200 step fountain fill. Autobackup time and other unrelated numeric boxes also display incorrect values, but fortunately this bug seems to only affect the numeric display, only causing panic, not actual damage.

✔ There is no LZW compression in TIF export filter in **Corel PhotoPaint 6**, despite a filter label to the contrary. The work-around (courtesy of Corel): find COREL60 \ CONFIG \ CORELFLT.INI, locate the [TIFF] section, modify the entry

```
Compressions2=-113, Packbits
```

to

```
Compressions2=-1, Packbits
```

Do the same for the entry under [CPT]. Next time you start Paint both packbits and LZW options will be available for TIF and .CPT files, and work correctly.

¥ The optimized for "smaller file size" feature does not work in **CorelDraw 6**. If you go Tools / Options / Advanced / Saving and Opening optimized for "smaller file size," the files generated may be the same size as when the option is not selected. The work-around: turning off "save presentation exchange data" helps make files a bit smaller.

¥ It is impossible to work with 16-color images in some circumstances in **Corel PhotoPaint 6**. If you open a 16-color bitmap that has a custom palette, not the "system" palette, save it with a new name, close and open again, Paint forces a conversion to "system" palette, and error diffusion dithering. The work-around: use 256-color palettes, or Photoshop or some other program to generate 16-color images.

¥ Converting between artistic and paragraph text in **CorelDraw 6** can change font sizes and placement. The work-around: after conversion, adjust font size and placement manually. Another option is the old cut-and-paste to convert between artistic and paragraph text.

✔ **CorelDraw 6**'s Wrap Paragraph Text attribute can generate GPFs if you draw an open curve with a bezier node (like a spiral) overlapping a text block, and you then right click on the spiral, and choose Properties / General / Wrap paragraph text. Click OK to accept... and you'll likely get an Invalid Page Fault. The work-around: close the curve before applying Wrap Paragraph Text.

✔The Bitmap Color Mask tolerance feature does not work correctly in **CorelDraw 6**. If you enter 100% as the tolerance, pick any color of a bitmap, apply it, and you should find all of the bitmap masked, but in fact only a portion of the image may be masked with this setting. Accoring to José Camara, "With some tests it is shown that the tolerance entered is being treated as RGB255 values, 100 selects + or - 100 units of the 0..255 range. In Paint and other locations it works as percentage (although 0..255 units gives better control and should be an option)." The work-around: enter values knowing they specify 0..255, not 0..100.

✔ If you find that text in **CorelDraw 6** looks "thorny" (no we didn't say "horny") when you zoom in a great deal, try setting

```
FontRasterizer=0
```

in your CORELAPP.INI

✔ **Corel PhotoPaint 6** reports incorrect DPI information for scans. For instance, if you make a scan at 200 DPI, Image / Info may report an incorrect value, not 200 DPI. In Trace, the same problem causes error messages asking for a scan over 200 dpi for OCR. The work-around:
use Image / Resample to change the DPI figure manually before saving in Paint.

✔ In **CorelDraw 6**, the Fit Text to Path rollup may disappear from screen. If you CTR-F to bring up Fit Text to Path rollup, click on the "tack" mini icon once, enabling AutoClose, then roll it up and down once, CTR-F will only bring the rollup onto the screen for a split second. To recover, delete CDRROL.CFG in your COREL60\DRAW directory so that it will be recreated the next time Draw starts. The work-around: do not use AutoClose in the Fit Text to Path rollup.

¥ In **CorelDraw 6,** the contour effect doesn't work except in very simple text (it will work with Avant Garde, but not with fonts with more nodes, like Bangkok). The work-around: use CorelDraw 5.

✔ In **CorelDraw 6** (unlike previous versions of CorelDraw), the Text rollup accepts only whole integer font sizes. Although the numeric box will accept and display a font size of 7.5, text info in the status bar will show 7.000. The work-around: use Text / Character to enter any fractional font size.

¥ In **CorelDraw 6**, the JPEG import filter loses the bottom line of graphics, which appears black.

¥ In **CorelDraw 6**, if you send one file to your printer and then switch to a second one (multitasking enabled), the Status Bar may disappear forever when the print job is completed. The work-around: restart CorelCraw to bring Status Bar back.

¥ In **CorelDraw 6**, fountain fills set for 256 levels of gray may export to TIF with only 101 levels of gray.

✔ Some data-heavy files (including those from Corel's own sampler CD such as 2MOROCCO.CDR) will print to a **Hewlett Packard LaserJet 4** from **CorelDraw 5**, but not CorelDraw 6, which generates a

```
21 Printer Overrun
```

error. This problem can occur on all PCL printers. The work-around: turn on Page Protection (in Printer Properties from the printers folder, not inside CorelDraw). However, this may cause a

`20 Memory Overflow`

error. And the work-around for this problem: you guessed it! Turn off Page Protection. The real solution is to add a bunch more RAM to your printer.

✔ WMF exports from **CorelDraw 6** cannot use long file names (the file may never be created if you use a long file name). The work-around: use old DOS-style names when exporting, and then rename later if necessary.

¥ **CorelDraw 6**'s fish eye lenses do not work on bitmaps.

✔ In **Corel PhotoPaint 6**, if you open a 24-bit color image, click Effects / Color Adjust / Color Replacer, then choose white as original color and any gray for the second one, you may get a

`Divide by Zero`

error in PICOR. The work-around: don't chose pure grays on both boxes.

¥ **CorelDRAW 6** will only export lines thicker than about .8mm properly into WMFs. If the line is thinner than that, it gets exported with no thickness at all. Corel Tech Support in Ireland has confirmed this and says a bug fix release will be available soon.

¥ Bullets in paragraph text can cause IPFs when saving in **CorelDraw 6**. This happens only if Tools / Options / Advanced / 'enable multitasking' is on. Turning it off "fixes" it, but may cause other problems, according to José Camara.

¥ Some fountain fills in **Corel PhotoPaint 6** may be incorrect. According to José Camara, you may reproduce the problem by creating a new 256 x 32 24-bit color image, and filling it with a fountain fill that is linear, horizontal, black (rgb 0,0,0) to white (rgb 255,255,255). In many places the color value in the resulting fill is not correct (i.e., different than the x coordinate). Position 0 is color 0, 255 is 255, but 148, for instance, has color 149,149,149. The work-around: in most cases the fill is acceptable, otherwise use **Photoshop**, **Photostyler** or even **Corel PhotoPaint 4** (**Corel PhotoPaint 5** reportedly suffers from the same problem).

¥ Toolbar customization in **CorelDraw 6**'s Multimedia Manager may cause IPFs if you open Multimedia Manager, select Tools / Customize / Toolbars, then try to drag one button to add to the current toolbar. Reportedly, an IPF occurs immediately, before you even release the mouse button.

¥ You may find that you can't edit **CorelDraw 6** Powerclips if they are not on page 1 of your document.

¥ In **CorelDraw 6** paragraph text, if you select Tools / Options / Advanced and enable multitasking, you may get IPFs when you try to save the file. The work-around: leave multitasking off.

¥ In **CorelDraw 6**, you may get an

`Condition #5002-TRAVTREE-0214`

error when changing from two-page to single-page view in a document with paragraph text, but it doesn't seem to affect the drawing.

¥ In **CorelTrace 6**, you may find you can't save in OS/2 BMP format. Instead you receive a
`Couldn't save image, make sure there is enough free disk space`
error message. The work-around: open in CorelPaint 6 and save as OS/2 BMP from there.

¥ In **CorelDraw 6** when you use CorelMove, you may find you can't edit an "actor" previously created with CorelDraw 5.

✔ When you try to print a document in **CorelDraw 4**, you may get a GPFin CDRGRFX40. In CorelDraw 5, the GPF may be in CDRGRFX50. The problem is that the path to the printer contains more than 19 characters. The work-around: shorten your path.

¥ **CorelDraw 4** may drop rotated ATM fonts when exporting a graphic to a bitmap format such as *.BMP, *.PCX, and *.TIF

✔ In **CorelDraw 4,** when printing to the Canon BJC600E printer, you may get GPFs unless you use the Windows 95 drivers.

¥ **Corel Ventura 4.2** will work under Windows 95, but the program starts slowly while reading in the system fonts and occasionally draws lines incorrectly while scrolling.

¥ According to Microsoft, **CorelDraw 3** may not run if installed on a hard disk of greater than 1 GB (and these days, what hard drive isn't?).

✔ When using a network printer with version of **CorelDraw 5** and prior, you must make sure the network path is associated with a printer port.

¥ **CorelPaint 6** reportedly has trouble maintaining the dpi of images either imported or exported in JPEG format. There is no work-around known at present.

¥ If you save an image in **CorelPaint 6** in JPEG format, then reopen it, you may find that the color in some areas has shifted.

¥ In **CorelPaint 6** if you try to scale objects across several pages, you may find that only the objects on page one actually scale. The work-around: according to José Camara, you have to entirely delete page one to scale page two, and so forth.

✔ After you enable Enhanced Metafile (EMF) spooling in Windows 95, applications like **Micrografx Designer 4.0** may not wrap text around objects properly. The work-around: disable EMF spooling with the following steps:
1. Click the Start button.
2. On the Settings menu, click Control Panel, then double-click the Printers icon.
3. In the Printers folder, double-click the icon for your printer.
4. Click the Printer menu, then click Properties.
5. Click the Detail tab, and then click the Spool Settings button.
6. Change the Spool Data Format from EMF to RAW.

✔ **Desktop Publisher for DOS,** from Spinnaker requires an HP II printer driver.

¥ Document files for Spinnaker's **Easy Working Desktop Publisher** lose their association when Windows 95 is installed by upgrading from an earlier version of Windows.

✔ To run **Bitstream's FaceLift 2.0** for Windows you need PNPDRVR.DRV in the Windows SYSTEM directory, with

```
display.org=pnpdrvr.drv
```

in SYSTEM.INI. The FaceLift version for **WordPerfect** does not have the same requirement.

✔ If you try to print a document using the Baskerville Old Face font or the New Caledonia TrueType font to a **Hewlett-Packard LaserJet 4Si,** you may get too many spaces between words. The work-around: choose the print TrueType fonts as graphics or download TrueType fonts as bitmaps options when printing.

¥ In **Hijaak 95**, the install program lets you specify a target location, but causes installation errors if you do not use the default location. Furthermore, the de-installation routines do not properly remove most of the registration entries.

¥ Many users report that after installing **Hijaak 95**, their Windows 95 systems run more slowly and sometimes won't shut down properly.

¥ Symantec **Just Write 2.0** may suffer occasional GPFs when pasting DDE information or when opening older DOC files.

¥ The tool bar may not display properly on Symantec **Just Write 2.0**.

¥ All Adobe PostScript Type 1 fonts are "lost" (i.e. don't appear) when printing from **Adobe PageMaker 5** to **Delrina WinFax 3**.

✔ If you lose your TrueType fonts in **Adobe PageMaker5** after installing Windows 95 ("The fonts are still on the control pallet like they are there, but the screen fonts look like Courier and print like Courier," observed one sufferer. All's fine in **Photoshop**, **CorelDraw**, **Access**, and all of my other applications. Only PM5 is doing this."), the problem is probably that you don't have the correct printer selected under Page Setup in PageMaker's File menu.

✔ When you try to use the Open Template addition in **PageMaker 5**, you may get an error like

```
Auto Template Generator 1.0/Out of
Memory: Script too long.
```

no matter what template you select and how much memory you have installed if you have a large number of fonts installed on your system (200 or more). The work-around: remove some fonts.

✔ After you install **Microsoft Office version 4.3**, the Font Assistant tool may not not recognize that there are any TrueType fonts installed because it doesn't know to look in Windows 95 registry for the information, instead of the [fonts] section of the WIN.INI. The work-around: reinstall TrueType fonts in Windows 95 as follows:

1. Click the Start button, point to Settings, and then click Control Panel.
2. Double-click the Fonts folder.
3. Click Install New Font on the File menu.
4. Select the drive and folder containing the new fonts, and then click the fonts in the List Of Fonts box.

¥ Microsoft acknowleges: "When you are using **Microsoft Paint**, you cannot use a palette that you saved with the Save Colors command to edit a 256-color bitmap. If you load the saved palette with the Get Colors command, choose a color from the saved palette, then use that color to edit the 256-color bitmap, the color that appears is different than the color you chose." There is no work-around at present.

¥ When you try to use the Color Eraser tool in **Microsoft Paint**, you will find that you can't change a bitmap if the image originated as a 24-bit image. The work-around: save the image as a 256-color or fewer image, and then erase.

✔ **PC Paintbrush 5+** from ZSoft requires MS-DOS Mode.

✔ **Photoshop 3.0** will run under Windows 95, although there are a couple of problems with using the Open and Save As dialogue boxes (you can't open TIFFs from within PhotoShop, but have to drag-and-drop them or double-click on them in Explorer to get them open). The best solution: upgrade to PhotoShop 3.04.

✔ If you get GPFs when trying to open or save a .TIF graphic with **PhotoShop 3.04**, the problem may be caused by a **Ray Dream Designer** plug-in named RDTIF.8BI. Deleting this file, and restarting PhotoShop 3.04 has cured the problem for some users.

✔ If you lose access to third party plugins like **Kai's Power Tools** after installing **PhotoShop 3.04,** we're sorry to report that you probably should try reinstalling both PhotoShop and the plugins.

✔ If you installed **PhotoShop 3.04** in a directory other than the default suggested by the setup program, and later you find that your scanner doesn't work, you might want to reinstall to the default directory, or `C:\WIN32APP\PHOTOSHOP`.

✔ **Kai's Power Tools** will not install correctly under **Photoshop 3.0** in Windows 95 because (according to Adobe), Microsoft left out the mechanism needed in Windows 95 that allows 32 bit applications to call 16 bit plugins. **PhotoShop 3.04** was released by Adobe in an attempt to workaround this (see the PSREADME.WRI file in the PhotoShop directory). A 32-bit version of KPT is in development and will be released soon.

✔ There is a problem with the "List of Files of Format Type" drop list field in **PhotoShop 3.0** running under Windows 95. If you open it and try to select anything, Photoshop may crash. This may happen with the Open, Open As, and Place dialog boxes. According to Compuserve Adobe Forum sysop Jeffrey Karasik, the work-around is:

1. When the Open dialog displays, you will notice that the 'File Name' field is highlighted. If you want to display TIFs, then type in *.tif and press Enter. You can then select the file you want in the left scroll box.
2. Open Photoshop and then minimize to the Task Bar. Then open Explorer and drag the TIF filename down to the Photoshop button on the Task Bar (don't drop it yet)... wait until Photoshop opens up and then drop in the main window. The nice thing about this method is that you can

drag up to 30 files at one time and drop them into **Photoshop**. They will all open. Photoshop can only have 30 images open at once. This bypasses the OPEN dialog Altogether. Just keep Explorer open in the background and when you want to open another image, minimize Photoshop and drag some more into Photoshop. This is fixed in PhotoShop 3.04.

✔ If you change the file format in the Save, Save As, Save As Copy dialogs in **PhotoShop 3.0**, you will get garbage after the file extension. The work-around: erase the garbage characters before saving the file. This is fixed in PhotoShop 3.04.

¥ Adobe **Photoshop 2.5** is incompatible with Windows 95, according to Microsoft.

✔ When you click the minimize button in Microsoft **PowerPoint 4.0** viewer in Windows 95, the viewer may close instead of minimize. To minimize the viewer, use the right mouse button to click the viewer button on the taskbar, and then click Minimize on the menu that appears.

¥ When you copy an image onto the Clipboard (using CUT, COPY, or Print Screen) and then paste that image into **Publisher's Paintbrush 2.0**, you may receive a GPF. GPFs may also occur in Publisher's Paintbrush 2.0 when you select an unavailable font. SoftKey suggets you upgrade to **PhotoFinish 3.0** which does not have this problem.

✔ If you get the error

```
This version of QuarkXPress can't be run
on this system [4]
```

it is probably caused by the fact you have a different language selected in the Regional Settings Control Panel than the language of **QuarkXPress** you are running. Open this Control Panel, and make sure you have English [United States] selected as the language if you are running US English QuarkXPress. Once you have made these change, restart Windows.

✔ There is a problem when running **QuarkXPress** under Windows95 in that only one page of fonts will display in the Style / Fonts menu. You can access all the fonts in the Measurements palette however. Reportedly, this will be fixed in the update to 3.32.

✔ In **QuarkXPress 3.31 release 5**, if you open or create a Library, the Library window appears without a title bar. So, the Library menu is not available and, more frustratingly, it is impossible to close the Library window. The work-around is to re-name the relevant library file(s). Then with a re-start, the situation is rectified.

✔ **QuarkXPress 3.3** will not run under Windows95, however if you install the update to 3.31 r5 you should be able to launch. This update is availble in the Quark Forum on Compuserve as W331R5.EXE.

✔ If you get an error like

```
Unable to Access Network
```

when running **QuarkXPress 3.31 release 5**, the problem may be due to a known conflict with the "IPX/SPX Compatible Transport - Dial Up Adapter" IF you aren't connected to a network. This driver is installed as part of the dial-up networking feature of Windows95. Remove this driver in the Network Control Panel, and you should be able to launch.

✔ To install additional fonts from **Microsoft TrueType Font Pack 2**, use the Fonts folder in Control Panel.

✔ **Two Thousand Fonts (Vol 1)** from Fantasia Concepts requires MS-DOS Mode. You will need to manually configure the program properties in Windows 95 to run in MS-DOS Mode.

¥ If you insert color images into **Visio 3.0**, white horizontal lines may appear on the screen and when the images are printed. The work-around: use a graphics utility other than Visio to convert the image from its original format to .BMP or .WMF format. Then insert the bitmap image into Visio.

✔ Colors in MS-DOS-based graphics programs running in a **Windows 95** window may appear weird unless you press ALT+ENTER to run the MS-DOS-based graphics program full-screen instead of in a window.

¥ If you cut a region in a **Windows 95 Paint** image selected with the Free-Form Select tool while you are zoomed in, the wrong region is cut. There is no work-around at present.

¥ If you try to jump to the end of a Rich Text Format file that is 4 Megs. or larger by meams of the CTRL+END key combination, **Windows 95 WordPad** may freeze. The only work-around is to use the scroll bar or PAGE DOWN key to move to the end of the file.

✔ If you find in **Word for Windows 6** that opaque drawing objects (like boxes covering text) appear clear when printed to a non-PostScript printer, you need to set TrueType fonts to print as graphics. To do this:

1. Click the Start button, point to Settings, and then click Printers.
2. Use the right (secondary) mouse button to click the desired printer.
3. Click Properties and then click the Fonts tab.
4. Click the Print TrueType Fonts As Graphics option.
5. Click OK to accept the changes.

✔ If you drag a Microsoft **Word for Windows 6** document icon to a Word application shortcut on the desktop, you may receive an error indicating that Word cannot open the document two separate times. This problem occurs because Word 6.0 for Windows recognizes only those files that conform to the 8.3 file specification. The work-around: rename the file to a name that contains no spaces and conforms to the 8.3 file specification.

✔ If the registration database entries for **Word for Windows 7** get corrupted, they can be restored by double clicking the supplied registration file, WINWORD7.REG installed by default in \MSOFFICE\WINWORD. However, although the file appears to contain registration entries, if you do the same with the corresponding Excel 95 file, EXCEL7.REG, you get an error message

```
The specified file is not a registry
script. You can only import registry
files.
```

✔ If you install the 16-bit version of Microsoft **Word for Windows 6.0** on a computer that already has the 32-bit version installed, you'll get the error:

`Can't Find SDM32.Dll`

The work-around: leave the 32-bit version of Microsoft Word 6.0 installed and uninstall the 16-bit version.

✔ If you copy information from one application and then try to paste it into Microsoft **Word for Windows NT** running under Windows 95, you will receive the following error:

Out of Memory

The work-around (such as it is): copy the information to WordPad, reselect it, choose Copy from the Edit menu, and then paste it into Word for Windows NT.

✔ You cannot load files using a universal naming convention (UNC) path specification when you are running Microsoft **Word 2.x for Windows.** The only work-around is to upgrade, or remove the Microsoft Client for NetWare Networks component.

✔ There is a patch to **WordPerfect for Windows 6.1** that fixes some "minor" problems in compatibility with Windows 95. The name of this file is POUPDT.EXE, and it is in library 17 of the WPFILES forum of CompuServe.

¥ When using **Wordperfect 6 for DOS** with Screen Extender under Windows 95, if you try and task switch, the system may crash. The problem only occurs in SVGA mode and can be avoided by re-loading Screen Extender in VGA mode.

✔ If you are suffering from a variety of problems including GPFs running **WordPerfect for Windows 6.1** under Windows 95, you should obtain a update patch from WordPerfect. The file is available as POUPDT.EXE on Compuserve's WPWIN Forum. This patch will not work on WordPerfect 6.0a for Windows.

✔ If you get the error

```
SPWIN20 caused a GPF in module
WTSU60.DLL.
```

when attempting to run the spell checker in **WordPerfect for Windows 6.1**, WordPerfect suggests several possible solutions:

1) Delete the WTSU60.DLL file and reinstall your Perfect Fit files.
2) Delete the WPSpeller group from the .BIF file.
3) Rename the Standard.WPT.
4) Rename the supplemental dictionary file.

¥ **WordPerfect 6.1 for Windows** goes in to a loop when trying to access a path that is more than 66 characters in length in Windows 95. There is a self extracting patch, POUPDT.EXE, available on Compuserve (GO WPFILES LIBRARY 17)

¥ Editing a **WordPerfect TextArt** image that was created in a font that is no longer installed on your system will cause TextArt to default to a font different from Arial. Arial is the default font that TextArt should look to when a specific font is not on the system anymore. According to Novell, this does not occur under Windows 3.1. There is no work-around at present.

✔ When starting **WordPerfect 6.1 for Windows,** if you get an error like

```
Cannot Initialize
```

the problem probably is that a .DLL file in the Windows directory has been damaged. The work-around: reinstall Windows 95.

✔ If after installing Windows 95, **WordPerfect for Windows 6.1** locks, or acts strange, there may be a problem with the information in the Windows 95 Registry. Novell suggests reinstalling all 16-bit applications, including WordPerfect.

¥ **WordPerfect 6.0 for Windows** may catch you in an infinite loop during the tutorial, according to Microsoft.

✔ For the mouse to work in **WordPerfect 6.0a for DOS**, the Exclusive setting must be enabled in program properties.

¥ If you run the 16 bit version of Lotus **WordPro 96** under Windows 95, the Text, Sort option will not display a scroll bar if you select the down arrow for the "Word" option. Because of this, you will not be able to sort using "Other," as you would if you were running under Windows 3.1.

¥ For those of you trying to use your scanners with **WordPro 96**, the Lotus Technical Support staff states that WordPro is not TWAIN-compliant.

✔ In **WordPro 96**, if you want to make a permanent change to your View Preferences, you now have to click the "Set Default" button, and make sure that you exit WordPro cleanly. In previous versions of **AmiPro**, View Preferences became the default as soon as you checked the option box.

✔ If you are running **WordPro 96** with 8 MB of memory or less, Lotus suggests you go to File, User Setup, WordPro Preferences and disable the option that says "Automatically save every...." Doing so will give you a large increase in program speed.

✔ Doug Benson, the Lotus WordPro product manager, reported during a CompuServe conference that a corrupt Monotype Sorts font shipped with **WordPro 96** sometimes causes problems with screen displays. The effect is to cause many applications which should use Bitmap Fonts (*.FON) to display text to use the corrupt font instead. Reported examples of this include: tool tips in Novell Perfect Office, status-line messages in Netscape and many different text fields in Font Spec Pro. The fix is to delete the font file from \WINDOWS\FONTS.

¥ The Lotus **WordPro** Tour, which is a product demonstration developed using **Lotus ScreenCam**, sometimes crashes when viewed at 256 colors. If you are having this problem, switch your video mode to 16 colors.

¥ **Microsoft Works version 2.0** Setup is not compatible with Windows 95.

✔ To use a network printer with **Lotus Write 2.0 for Windows,** make sure the network path is associated with a printer port. Windows 95 Help automatically provides information.

Chapter 7 -- Working With Numbers

Gilda Radner lives!

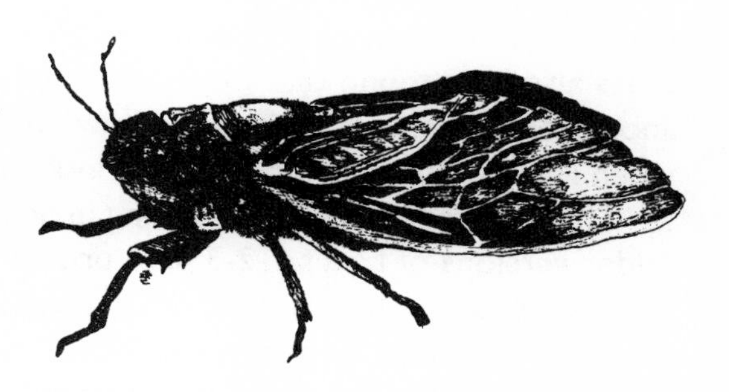

Remember Emily Littela of *Saturday Night Live* fame? As played by Gilda Radner, her specialty was to get all worked up over what she thought was some great issue, only to find out that it was all a simple misunderstanding.

Well, frankly there is a fair amount of that going on right now in the realm of spreadsheets, databases, and personal finance software — what we have grouped together here under the rubric of "Working with Numbers."

The support forums on Compuserve and America Online are filled with gripes from users, yet many of the complaints you hear about really don't relate to these programs at all — they have to do with Windows 95 installation issues (see chapter 1), hardware compatibility issues (see chapter 3) and conflicts with various utilities (see chapter 2).

When you strip all of this away, what you are left with is a host of user interface problems. For instance, both Microsoft FoxPro and Borland dBase have all manner of difficulty with such routine tasks as minimizing, maximizing and closing windows. Also in this category is the bizarre "growth" of user-defined dialog boxes in Novell Quattro Pro. In some cases, there will battles for screen real estate between the new taskbar in Windows 95 and existing tool and menu bars in the programs.

Somewhat more aggravating (and somewhat more serious) are the printing and date difficulties that have emerged in Intuit's Quicken and QuickBooks. Quattro Pro users also have found that there are some odd formating anomalies for essential things like how currency is displayed when running the program under Windows 95.

There are some time-consuming problems as well. Older versions of Lotus 1-2-3 have problems loading spreadsheets that contain graphs or queries. Workarounds for these problems have been developed by users, but in many cases they need to be done any time you open one of these files. The problems don't show up in the latest version 5 for Windows.

On the serious end of the scale, there are some bugs which produce inaccurate calculations. The new 32-bit Microsoft Excel for Windows 95 is the victim of the most flashy of these. They include errors when calculating or using certain large powers of 2 (raising 2 to the 47th, 48th, or 49th power), math errors when links across multipage spreadsheets are used, problems when doing a high num-

Bug/Fix Success Rates for Publishing

The bug/fix success rate for spreadsheets, databases and personal accounting software is already above the average for Windows 3.x. and should rise even higher.

Biggest Number Problem

Errors that affect the accuracy of calculations and queries are of course the most serious problems that can afflict software of this sort, and there are a few to be aware of in Excel.

Biggest Surprise

The amount of smoke (if not fire) that has surrounded FoxPro.

ber of iterations, and an old favorite: in Excel 7 — as with Excel 5 before it — if you try to enter the number 1.40737488355328 into any cell, you will get the value 0.64. Go figure, as they say.

The good news is that there are fixes or work-arounds for many of these problems. The major vendors are clearly working hard to stomp the serious bugs in calculation software running under Windows 95, and we expect the situation here to improve steadily. For instance, a patch for

Excel 7 has already been released by Microsoft to deal with the powers of 2 issue.

We aren't quite there yet, but before long we expect Emily would say, "Never mind."

Windows 95 Numbers Bug & Fix List

1-2-3, Access, Excel, dBase, Quattro, Quicken, Quickbooks and much more...

¥ Versions of Lotus **1-2-3** prior to version 3.0 are not supported by Windows 95 Quick View.

✔ Lotus **1-2-3 3.0** requires MS-DOS Mode.

✔ Sean Acton of London, England, reports that he has problems opening up any Lotus **1-2-3 for Windows 4** spreadsheets that contain graphs. The error message is `MAIN123W caused a general protection fault in module L1WDQA.DLL at 0010:00000090.`
If he creates a new spreadsheet with the same number of worksheets as the old file, and then combines the files, he

---

Bug & Fix List Legend: The symbol ¥ denotes bugs, incompatibilities and other difficulties. The symbol ✔ denotes problems which have either been fixed, or resolved with some sort of acceptable work-around. Products are listed in alphabetical order.

can access his data. The fix from Lotus was a suggestion to upgrade to version 5.

✔ There is a problem with **1-2-3 4.x** spreadsheets that contain queries. If you try to open these spreadsheets under Windows 95. When loading files that contain query tables a GPF will occur in L1WDQA.DLL. After closing the error, you will not be able to restart 1-2-3 without restarting Windows first. Bud Zielinski of Barefoot Bay, Florida, was able to come up with a fix: Start 1-2-3 4.0 and create a worksheet with some data and do a query on that data. Save the file and close it. Then you will able to load your files that contain query tables. Other users with this problem report that the fix works.

✔ In Microsoft **Access 2.0**, when you create a database and accept the default name, and then you create a second database while the first is still open, you may receive the message:

```
System Error: The file you are trying to
open is already in use by another pro-
gram. Quit the other program, and then
try again.
```

The work-around: rename the first database before you open the second database.

✔ The "File Send" command option in Lotus **Approach** does not work if the file MSMAIL.INI is missing from your \WINDOWS directory. The workaround is to create an empty file with that name and place it in \WINDOWS.

✔ The Lotus **Approach** forum on CompuServe has been flooded with complaints about extra blank pages being printed out between the pages of reports by people running Approach under Windows 95. Lotus has not reported a fix, but Kurt Werner of Appleton, Wisconsin, says he solved the problem by going to the [Compatibility] section of WIN.INI, finding the line that says:

```
APPROACH=0x0004
```

and putting a semi-colon in front of the line to de-activate it. At least three others with this problem and who have tried the fix report that it works for them too.

✔ Patrick Kennedy (Borland) has confirmed that **dBase 5 for Windows** refuses to open DBF files if you use a dBASE III Plus file (w/memo) in dBASE IV or dBase 5 for DOS. The workaround: in dBASE IV copy to a new file, thereby making it a dBASE IV file type. If compatibility needs to be maintained across III, IV and 5, use COPY TO newfile TYPE dbmemo3

✔ When running **dBASE 5.0** under Windows 95, right-clicking in Browse on the Right-Edge of the screen can cause a flickering property window or hangup. This is fixed in the latest release of **Visual dBASE**.

✔ When running **dBASE 5.0** under Windows 95, It is not possible to run a program located in a directory with a long file name. This is fixed in the latest release of **Visual dBASE**.

✔ When running **dBASE 5.0** under Windows 95, Minimizing or Maximizing a form can kill the events. This is fixed in the latest release of **Visual dBASE**.

¥ Borland has confirmed there is an incompatibility between **Visual dBASE 5.5**, **Lantastic 6.0** and Windows 95 which causes Page Fault Errors when trying to access files on a Network Drive. There is currently no fix available, but Borland and Artisoft are collaborating to solve the problem.

✔ Borland **dBase Debugger for Windows 5.0** may cause a GPF in module DBWDEBUG.EXE when you load a program. **Visual dBase 5.5** does not have this problem.

✔ During the installation of Computer Associates **CA-dBFast 1.7c and 2.0,** the installation program pauses while attempting to create the program group and displays the message:

```
Installation program cannot communicate
with Program Manager.
```

Clicking OK results in an "installation successful" dialog box. CA-dBFast works fine, but the program group folder is not created. The work-around: run CA-dBFast from My Computer or Windows Explorer, or create a shortcut icon for CA-dBFast.

¥ **Easy Expense Reports 1.0** from Outlook Software gets weird when you preview a report on the screen. Once you open that window it won't close. The installation message that SHARE has to be loaded in AUTOEXEC.BAT isn't much help since SHARE is not used by Windows 95.

¥ If you have established shortcut keys in **Ecco 3.0** such as CTRL-ALT-E, they will initially work but will not maximize Ecco once the program has been minimized.

✔ When you make a Microsoft **Excel 5.0** window containing a minimized workbook shorter in height, the minimized workbook may become hidden from view. The work-around: click Arrange Icons on the Window menu. This places the icons at the bottom edge of the window. And, they remain there when you resize the window again.

¥ Several users have reported that a bug previously reported to Microsoft in **Excel 5**, has not been fixed in the latest version 7 for Windows 95. Try entering 1.40737488355328 into any cell -- bizarrely the cell fills with the value 0.64, unless you start the entry with "=." Other numbers fill the cells correctly without the need to enter the equals sign.

✔ When you try to open a file in a 16-bit version of Microsoft **Word for Windows** or Microsoft **Excel**, you may receive the following error message:

`This file could not be found <Filename>.`

These error messages occur when you try to open a file whose 8.3 filename contains a space. The space can be created in the filename by a 16-bit Windows-based program that uses a Windows 95 common dialog box, but the filename is invalid because the 8.3 filename format does not allow spaces. The work-around is to rename the file without the space.

¥ When you drag a Microsoft **Excel** worksheet object to a WordPad document, the worksheet's properties are lost, and only the worksheet's text is moved to the WordPad document. At present, there is no work-around for this problem.

¥ There is a bug in **Excel 7** that can cause math errors in multiple-page spreadsheets. The problem occurs when numbers are linked to each other across different pages of a spreadsheet: changing one number does not update the second one as it should. Microsoft is reportedly working on a fix.

✔ **Excel 7** has a problem with three particular numbers. These numbers are 2 raised to the 47th, 48th, and 49th power. The values of these numbers may change unexpectedly when they are entered into a worksheet cell, or are calculated by a formula. There is a patch file called WE1255.EXE, that will correct these problems. This file is available in the Microsoft Excel spreadsheet forum on CompuServe.

✔ Two macros installed by Delrina's **WinFax** program, MSEXCEL4.XLM and MSEXCEL5.XLM into the XLSTART directory, are incompatible with **Excel 7**. If you start Excel 7 with these macros present, you may get a runaway macro that opens 100 worksheets. Delrina should be releasing updates to these macros soon.

✔ If you performed a "Minimum" installation of **Excel 7**, then it is possible that the Visual Basic help files were not installed from the Office CD to your hard drive. This will result in the message that:

```
C:\Program Files\Common Files\Microsoft
Shared\VBA\VBAen.hlp file cannot be
found.
```

Copying this file from the CD and placing it in the listed folder will not update the registry, so that Excel still will not find the file. You will have to go to the Control Panel, select the Add/Remove Programs icon, and restart the Office setup program. Within the Install Excel option, highlight "Online Help and Sample Files." Then make sure that "Online Help for Visual Basic" is selected. While adding this option, make sure you do not unselect any previously installed option.

¥ **Excel 7** will not import Novell Quattro Pro worksheets in the WB2 format.

✔ If you try to open a file with a long file name that contains spaces, **Excel 7** will open but you will get an error message for each word in the long file name. The work-around:
1. Double-click on "My Computer", and then select View, Options.
2. Go to File Types, click on Excel Worksheet in the Registered File Type box, and select Edit. Select Actions, Open, Edit. Where it says "Application Used to Perform Action" add a space and "%1" to the line. (Include the quotation marks.)
3. Then click on OK, and then close the two windows. A similar problem affects **Word 7**, but not the other apps in the **Office 95** Suite.

¥ If you use Windows 95 QuickView to view an **Excel** file that contains graphs, the graphs may not be displayed properly. This is especially true if there are multiple chart types, such as line charts and bar charts. The charts may be converted to incorrect types. As of now, there is no fix for this problem.

¥ Steve Leary of Richmond, California, notes that, in **Excel 7**, if you select Display Properties, Settings, Font Size, Custom and set your display to 75% you get an optimal WYSIWYG for Word processing and DTP, but in Excel you get what look like 2D black on white button bars. Lori Turner of Microsoft Technical Support has confirmed this.

¥ John LaTour of Microsoft Technical Support says that they have seen many problems with **Excel 7** (and **Office 95**) and **Windows NT** when running the Win95 shell. The shell is presently beta, and he does not recommend that you use it.

✔ Phil Scarbrough of Draper, Utah has uncovered a bug in the recalculation function of **Excel 7.** Go to Tools, Options, Calculation and enable Iteration. Set Max Iterations to 100 and Maximum Change to .00001. Put the following into the worksheet: Cell B1=100; Cell A2=10%; Cell B2= A2*B3; Cell B3=B1+B2. Cell B3 should recalculate to 111.1111111. Change cell B1 to 1,000. Cell B3 recalculates to 1111.11111. Change cell B1 back to 100. Cell B3 does not recalculate. After confirming this problem, a Microsoft engineer called him to report a fix. The solution is a simple formula that needs to be entered to the work sheet to force Excel to iterate. This formula can be added anywhere in the work sheet and can be hidden if necessary. If you have several work sheets open, it only needs to be in any one open work sheet. For example, use cell A1 to enter the formula =A1+1. This formula will force Excel to iterate the number of iterations set in the Maximum Iterations box (Tools + Options + calculation) every time a formula is recalculated. Phil has tried this out on some of his worksheets that require iteration and reports that it seems to work fine.

✔ In Microsoft **FoxPro for Windows 2.5 and 2.6**, the Close button (the button displaying an "x" in the upper-right corner of the window) is either dim or does not appear at all. The work-around: click on the icon on the left of the windows menu bar. Then you get a drop down menu that allows you to maximze, minimize and close.

✔ After you install **Maximizer for Windows 1.1** in Windows 95, it cannot find its databases because Maximizer for Windows does not recognize network paths that use the universal naming convention (UNC). The work-around:

1. Create a persistent connection to the machine that contains the Maximizer databases.
2. Open the MAXWIN.INI file and change

```
[Directory]
DBases=\\<MachineName>\<ShareName>\<PathName>
```

so that it reads

```
[Directory]
DBases=<x>:\<path to the Maximizer data-
bases>
```

where <x>: is the drive letter specified in step 1.

✔ When you type the amount of a transaction in **Money**, you may receive the error message:

```
Error: 'xxx.xx' is an invalid amount.
```

The work-around:

1. Click Settings, and then Control Panel.
2. Double-click Regional Settings.
3. Select the Number tab.
4. In the Decimal symbol box, verify that the decimal separator is a period. If you are unsure change it to a period.
5. Click Apply, choose OK. Close the Control Panel.

✔ Lotus **Notes** does not recognize Uniform Naming Conventions (UNC) paths, and therefore cannot find the printer if you are using one. The work-around: make sure the network path is associated with a printer port:
1. Click the Start button, point to Settings, and then click Printers.
2. In the Printers dialog box, using the right mouse button, click the icon for the printer you use, and then click Properties.
3. In the Properties box for the printer, click the Details tab, then click Capture Printer Port .
4. In the Capture Printer Port dialog box, select the port the printer is connected to, and then type the path to the printer.
5. In the Lotus Notes Printer Setup dialog box, select the printer you captured.

¥ Lotus **Notes Windows Server 3.15 and 3.2** both have had "minor problems" which are not found with 3.2b.

¥ Borland has confirmed a problem with **Paradox 5** under Windows 95. When selecting a portion of data the screen does not show the highlight properly. The copy and/or cut commands work, but it can be confusing not to be able to see the highlighted selection.

¥ Loss of **Paradox for Windows 5.0** background images can occur when you upgrade to Windows 95. Brian Bushay (Team Borland) confirms that this is a known problem, caused by last minute changes Microsoft made to Windows, and is not helped by reinstalling Paradox (sorry).

✔ If you get a message

```
Cannot find the NETWARE.DLL that
paradox.exe needs to run
```

when launching **Paradox** under Windows 95, Brian Bushay (Team Borland) suggests checking that no other versions of the file NWCALLS.DLL exist, except for the version which ships with Paradox (dated 1/2/93), which should be in the \Windows\System directory, and which does not require the NETWARE.DLL.

✔ You may encounter problems printing reports using OPAL code with **Paradox for Windows 5.0** under Windows 95. All reports print in Portrait orientation even though the code is written to print the report in Landscape. The workround is to use the OPAL code:

```
rp.open("your.rsl",WinStyleDefault+WinStyleHidden)
rp.print()
rp.close()
```

¥ When using **Paradox for Windows** under Windows 95, if you use cut and paste to copy information from the Help file a Borland copyright notice will be pasted along with your information. The only workround is to delete this text.

✔ Microsoft **Profit 1.0b** must have the network path mapped to a printer port if you are using a network printer.

✔ In Novell's **Quattro Pro 6.0 for Windows**, if a file icon is dragged to a printer icon, the file loads, but is not printed. To correct this, change the value in the Registry of Hkey_Classes_Root\QuattroPro.Notebook.6

```
\shell\print\ddeexec to
{FileOpen "%1"}{Print ?}{FileClose 0}.
```

To install to a NetWare server from a computer running Windows 95, first add
`secondnet.drv=netware.drv`
in the [boot] section of SYSTEM.INI.

¥ Barry Schnur, the sysop of the Novell Quattro Pro forum, reports that he and other sysops from Novell have been having problems importing **Quattro Pro** WB1 files into Excel 95, even though this format is supported by Excel 95. Frequent GPFs are said to result, even from fairly simple spreadsheets.

¥ While running under Windows 95, **Quattro Pro 6.0** spreadsheets with cells displayed as currency may display as "$,Quattroxx.xx" where xx.xx is the correct value. To fix this, first, restart Quattro Pro. Then use Property, Application, International, Currency and edit the format or chose Windows default. This should resolve the problem.

¥ **Quattro Pro 6.02** dialog boxes seem to grow when running under Windows 95. Novell Technical Support has verified that the boxes get 2 pixels higher and wider each time they are executed, as well as shifting one pixel up and left. If you add the following link to the dialog boxes
```
"ON Init SET xxx,yyy,www,hhhh TO
MyDialog Dimensions"
```
they should stay the same size.

✔ There is a battle for screen real estate if you are running **QuickBooks 3 CD** and Windows 95. The "Business Center" icon for QuickBooks will cover up the "Minimize" icon in the far right corner. According to Intuit, this will be redesigned in future releases. For now, if you want to minimize, point to the Title Bar and right-click with the mouse. This will bring up a drop-down menu where you can choose "Minimize."

✔ If you are running **QuickBooks for Windows 2** with QuickPay under Windows 95, and you get the error message

```
Qbw  An error has occurred in your pro-
gram . . close/ignore
```

you may need to run the MKCOMPAT program that was included in Windows 95. This program helps some **Windows 3.x** applications run under Windows 95. To run the program in Windows 95:

1. Select Start, Run, and type MKCOMPAT.
2. Now select File, Choose Program, and enter QBW.EXE.
3. Next, select Lie About Printer Device Mode(QBW ver2.0 only) and Win 3.1 Style Controls.
4. Finally, select File, Save and close down MKCOMPAT.

This will not change your QBW.EXE file, but adjusts how Windows 95 deals with it.

✔ In Intuit **QuickBooks 2.0 for Windows**, a GPF can occur when opening a new invoice window. According to Intuit, pressing "ignore" will allow the user to continue using the program. Some users report success in solving this problem by selecting the "3.1 style controls" option in the MKCOMPAT program.

✔ In **Quicken Home Inventory 3 for Windows, Release 7**, you may get a GPF in the List View when adding an Item that is not on the Suggested Item List. Intuit has released a fix, which is available on Compuserve (QH13R8.ZIP in library 2 of GO INTUIT).

✔ If you have printing problems using **Quicken 3 or 4** under Windows 95, in most cases it is because your print preferences were overwritten during the installation of Windows 95. You will have to go back in Checks, Setup, as well as rechoose all of your other print options. They are reported to work, they just need to be set again.

✔ There have been a lot of worries over "grayed-out" buttons in **Quicken 4**. According to Intuit Technical Support, "With WIN95, the non active buttons will look considerably different. This is not a bug, it is just the way the operating system working in unison with Quicken displays these buttons. ... [W]hen they are active, they look normal."

✔ There is a conflict between **Quicken 4 CD** and Microsoft's **Intellitype Manger 1.1** for Serial Mouse and Natural Keyboard. When trying to load Quicken, you will get a

```
Segment Load Failure.
```

The work-around: according to Linda Kretin of Toledo, OH, right-click on the Point32 button on the Task Bar, and close this program before you run Quicken.

✔ There is a conflict with **Quicken 4 release 7 CD** version and the Intellipoint 1.10 driver from Microsoft. It could cause the error message

```
QW caused a segment not present fault in
module QW.EXE at 0094:000007d0.
If this happens, you should request
version 1.11 of the driver.
```

Chapter 8
-- Windows 95 (Itself)

Watch those speed bumps!

So now you have Windows 95 installed and running, hopefully with the minimum of unresolved problems. You've managed to get all your old applications working at least as well as they did under Windows 3.11.

You had to scrap a few that wouldn't work at all, replace some with new 32-bit versions, and along the way you spent more money than you ever expected to, upgrading your hardware to cope with the increased strain that Windows 95 put on it.

You're probably beginning to wonder whether it was all worth it. Well, Relax! Now's the time to start enjoying your new operating system and make its many nifty features work for you. Time to do some cruisin'.

Be aware, however, that there are a couple of speed bumps in Windows 95 / MS-DOS 7 itself that can rattle your teeth if you hit them blind.

For instance:

• There is a bug in Windows 95's OLE 2.0 object linking and embedding technology that can cause data from previously deleted files to show up in new files created by some Windows 95 applications, including Microsoft Office 95.

• The backup applet included with Windows 95 has a number of problems, including not supporting dedicated controller boards or SCSI based streamers. (Fortunately, a free upgrade which overcomes some of the problems has just been released — see listings below).

• XCOPY32 does not prompt you before overwriting files as the old MS-DOS XCOPY command did (how's that for progress?). Similarly, XCOPY32 does not have the ability to copy the attributes of folders.

• If you put too many items in a Windows 95 folder, you won't be able to access them all from Start because Windows 95 doesn't have the ability to scroll to the right to view items off the screen.

• If you try to use certain extended ANSI characters, such as code 147 (opening double quotation mark), 148 (closing quotation mark), or 151 (em-dash), you'll find that Windows 95's screen fonts can't display them properly.

And then there is the problem of Windows 95 Registry corruption, which could become the Achille's heel of Windows 95. The registration database consists of SYSTEM.DAT and USER.DAT, two files which are destined to grow rapidly to multimegabyte size on most systems.

Bug/Fix Success Rates for Windows 95

The bug/fix success rate for Windows 95 itself is already a very respectable 69 percent, and we expect it to rise even higher.

Biggest Windows 95 Problem

We believe that corruption of the Windows 95 Registry -- either by poorly designed installation programs or virus like sabatuers – will prove to be the biggest problem for Windows 95.

Biggest Surprise

Unlike it's old MS-DOS forebare, XCOPY32 doesn't prompt the user before overwriting files.

Careless editing of the Registry can bring Windows 95 to its knees, and worst of all, such a result could just as easily be achieved with a poorly written commercial install program, to say nothing of rogue viruses and the like.

Some users have already described problems that appear to be related to mystery corruption of the registry: programs or features that worked fine after initial installation suddenly stop working, change in functionality or just plain disappear for no obvious reason.

Such difficulties are very hard to nail down, but they can usually be fixed by reinstalling or re-registering the application concerned. It may be that this procedure becomes the first line of defense in dealing with Windows 95 complaints.

Windows 95 (Itself) Bug & Fix List

Backup, XCOPY32, DriveSpace, WinHelp, ScanDisk and much more...

✔ **Colorado Memory Systems** (CMS) has released a free upgrade to the Windows 95 Backup applet, which addresses some of the known problems and includes a scheduler, support for SCSI tape streamers and Colorado controller boards, as well as extra tape tool features such as security erase, unerase and rename. The file, CBW95.EXE, is available from CompuServe (PCVENF, Library 11). If you make backups to floppy disks, however, be warned that CMS has removed support for this backup medium.

¥ Here's a little bomb Microsoft dropped on Corel. The WTBackup (version 1.13) tool that is shipped with the **CorelSCSI** package is incapable of performing a complete system backup of Windows 95 systems. "This behavior is

---

Bug & Fix List Legend: The symbol ¥ denotes bugs, incompatibilities and other difficulties. The symbol ✔ denotes problems which have either been fixed, or resolved with some sort of acceptable work-around. Products are listed in alphabetical order.

caused by new features included with Windows 95. Contact Corel about possible upgrades to the WTBackup tool," says Microsoft.

✔ If you install **Windows 95** on a computer that already has the Linux operating system installed, Windows 95 may nuke the Linux boot manager (LILO, or Linux Loader), rendering Linux inoperable. To correct this problem, you can either

1. Restart the computer using a bootable Linux floppy disk.
2. Run the LILOCONFIG program from the floppy drive, or if LILO was installed to the superblock, use the FDISK command to activate the Linux partition.

¥ **Logitech Multiscope Debugger** does not start when running under Windows 95. Multiscope must be updated to run under Windows 95. Contact Logitech for update information.

✔ Microsoft Backup (from **MS-DOS 6** and above) requires MS-DOS Mode. The program is replaced by the Windows 95 Backup program, although it can be used to restore previous backup sets.

✔ Microsoft acknowledges that running under Windows 95, **Microsoft Quick C for Windows 1.0** does not run a program after it has compiled it. The work-around: upgrade Quick C for Windows to Microsoft Visual C++ 1.0 Standard Edition or Visual C++ 1.5 Professional Edition.

¥ You cannot install PC-NFSpro 1.1 from **Sun Microsystems** in Windows 95. If you were running PC-NFSpro before you installed Windows 95, you won't be able to any longer.

¥ After you install Windows 95 to a compressed **SuperStore version 2.04** boot disk, the F4 boot feature (to start your previous version of MS-DOS) does not work. According to Microsoft, there is no way to work around this behavior.

¥ If you press the <ESACAPE> key accidentally whilst **Windows 95** Backup is trying to detect and configure your Tape Hardware (and the message dialog is on screen), you may encounter the error message:

```
MS Backup has encountered a serious
error in Task Manager. Quit MS Backup
and all running programs and then try
again. Quit MS Backup and all running
programs and then try again.
```

Come again? Yes, the dialog actually does repeat itself that way. Clearly a little Dialog Box tidying up is in order!

¥ Backup for **Windows 95** comes without a DOS Restore module or the ability to run from your choice of either Windows or DOS (like the Windows 95 Setup program). This incredible oversight means that if you suffer a catastrophic data loss or damaged hard disk that requires reformatting, instead of merely running the Backup program from DOS, your first step will have to be a fresh install of Windows 95 before you can restore your last full backup.

✔ **Windows 95** appears to make no attempt to optimize conventional DOS memory when it is installed. You could end up with as little as 576K free conventional memory in a DOS box for games and other DOS programs or 580K in MS-DOS compatibility mode (even less if you have to load other real-mode drivers before running Win95). This is because, by default, Win95 does not create Upper Memory Blocks (UMBs). Win95 claims not to need AUTOEXEC.BAT or CONFIG.SYS files and indeed without them HIMEM.SYS is loaded automatically. But EMM386.EXE is not, and although not needed for EMS support (since Win95 can provide it automatically), without it UMB's are not used. By including a line such as

```
DEVICE=C:\WINDOWS\EMM386.EXE NOEMS
```

in your CONFIG.SYS file it is possible to maximize memory for your games and DOS programs to as much as 620K.

✔ **Microsoft Plus!** installs JPEG inport filters into \WINDOWS\MSAPPS\GRPHFLT directory, ignoring the fact, if you already have MS Office 95 installed this will likely have put its graphic import filters into \PROGRAM FILES\COMMON FILES\GRPHFLT (or if you let it - one level deeper still -- into \PROGRAM FILES\COMMON FILES\MICROSOFT SHARED\GRPHFLT !!). The fix, if you are feeling brave, is to move the JPEG files across and manually change the Path String in the System Registry at: HLM / Software / Microsoft / Shared Tools / Graphic Filters /Import/JPEG. If, after installing MSPlus! you dont like the new startup screen (with the jazzy MS-Plus! logo added), you can return to the original Win95 logo by deleting the file "LOGO.SYS" in the root directory (C:\).

¥ The button you press to shut down **Windows 95** is labeled "Start."

¥ If you try to change the file type of a document via **Windows 95** Explorer (say from .TXT to .DOC), the old file extension isn't changed — the new is just added on, producing invalid file names like DOCUMENT.TXT.DOC.

¥ You can not create dynamic links to shortcuts across drives in **Windows 95**.

¥ **Window 95** Explorer hides some file extensions by default. For instance, .TIF files display their full name, but .EXE files do not.

✔ If you receive an error message stating that a particular program requires **Windows 3.1** or later when starting under Windows 95, the problem may be that the application is confused when it checks the version number of Windows 95. As a possible work-around, Microsoft suggests the following:

1. Start Windows Explorer.
2. Open the folder containing the executable file you want to run.
3. Use the right mouse button to click the executable file, then click Quick View on the menu that appears. Note the module name in the Quick View window.
4. Use any text editor (such as WordPad) to open the WIN.INI file.
5. In the [Compatibility] section of the file, add the following line

```
<ModuleName>=0x00200000
```

where <ModuleName> is the name you noted in step 3.

6. Save and close the WIN.INI file.
7. Try running the program again.

NOTE: If the module name is INSTALL or SETUP, remove the change to the WIN.INI file after you have successfully installed the program. The presence of this statement can cause other installation programs to fail.

✔ If you change the screen font in an MS-DOS window to a TrueType font, but the font on the screen doesn't change, the problem may be solved by running the application in text mode (if it has such a mode) or running it in full screen mode by pressing ALT+ENTER to run the MS-DOS app in **Windows 95**'s full screen mode.

✔ If you rename or move the original My Briefcase to a different folder, and then try to send a file to Briefcase by clicking the file with the right mouse button and then clicking Send To Briefcase on the menu that appears, you receive the following error message:

```
The Briefcase cannot be opened because
the disk is inaccessible.
Verify that the disk is accessible.
```

The problem is that the shortcut in the <Windows>\SendTo folder does not point to an existing Briefcase. The work-around is:

1. Open the <Windows>\SendTo folder, where <Windows> is the folder containing **Windows 95**.
2. Use the right mouse button to click the My Briefcase shortcut, then click Properties on the menu that appears.
3. Click the Shortcut tab, and then change the target to point to an existing Briefcase.

✔ When you double-click a **Windows 95** desktop shortcut linked to CONTROL.EXE to start Control Panel, there is a delay as long as 90-seconds, accompanied by intense hard disk churning before Control Panel appears. The work-around is to Start Control Panel from My Computer instead of from the shortcut to CONTROL.EXE. To launch Control Panel from My Computer, double-click My Computer on the desktop, then double-click Control Panel.

✔ If you have too many items in a **Windows 95** folder, you will not be able to access them all, since Windows 95 does not have the capacity to scroll to the right to see items off the screen. This can occur when you click an item on the Start menu, and a menu covers the entire screen and wraps off the right side of the screen. You cannot access any items on the menu that are not visible, and there does not seem to be any way to remove the menu without clicking an item on it. The work-around is to use either Windows 95 Explorer or My Computer to view the folder

✔ If you find that the FORMAT and DELETE commands do not work in **Windows 95**, the problem may be a corrupted or accidentally deleted DRVSPACX.VXD. To restore this file, open a DOS Windows and type

```
extract /l <drive
letter>:\windows\system\iosubsys
<drive letter>:\win95_11.cab
drvspace.vxd
```

where <drive letter> indicates the letter designating the drive containing the floppy disk or CD-ROM. Then restart the system.

✔ If after installing **Windows 95** and restarting the system, you get the following error message:

```
Incorrect MS-DOS version
Enter the name of Command Interpreter
(e.g., C:\WINDOWS\COMMAND.COM)
```

the problem is that SETVER.EXE is being loaded in the CONFIG.SYS file and has a setting indicating that COMMAND.COM should look for a version of MS-DOS earlier than 7.0. The work-around:

1. Boot the system with the Windows 95 Startup disk and rename SETVER.EXE by typing:

```
ren setver.exe setver.old
```

2. Remove the Windows 95 Startup disk from drive A and shut down and restart the system. 3. Then click the Start button, point to Programs, and then click MS-DOS Prompt, change to the Windows directory and rename the SETVER.EXE file again by typing:

```
ren setver.old setver.exe
```

4. Now type:

```
setver command.com /d
```

5. Finally, restart the computer to make the SETVER changes take effect.

✔ When you are using a real-mode driver (DRVSPACE.BIN or DBLSPACE.BIN) and you try to access a file on a DriveSpace or DoubleSpace compressed drive in **Windows 95**, the computer may stop freeze. With a protected-mode driver (DRVSPACX.VXD), you may receive the error message Read Fault. The problem is that you are trying to access information stored in one or more bad clusters on your hard drive The fix suggested by Microsoft: With the protected-mode DriveSpace driver loaded, run ScanDisk for Windows and click the Thorough option button in the Type Of Test box. Test both the system and data areas on the compressed drive, as well as on the host drive.

¥ If you use **Windows 95** to access a network drive that is larger than 2 gigabytes (for example, an NTFS or FAT volume shared by a Windows NT server), Windows 95 may report only 2 GB of disk space for the network drive. If the network drive is larger than 2 GB and has more than 2 GB of available disk space, Windows 95 reports 2 GB of total disk space, 2 GB of available disk space, and 0 bytes of used disk space. If the network drive has less than 2 GB of available disk space, Windows 95 reports the available disk space correctly.

✔ If you run Microsoft Disk Defragmenter a second time immediately after defragmenting your hard disk, you may notice it reports that a small percentage of fragmentation still exists. The reason is that Disk Defragmenter creates a database of files and their associated clusters which can itself cause a small degree of fragmentation. Microsoft says, "Disk Defragmenter is designed to work this way; therefore, this behavior requires no workaround."

✔ If you receive the following error messages when you run DriveSpace:

```
Files required to manage your compressed
drive(s) are missing on drive <x>. To
restore these files, copy the MINI.CAB
file from your Windows 95 Setup Disk 1
or CD-ROM into your Windows directory.
The next time you run DriveSpace, the
missing files will be restored.
ID Number: DRVSPACE575
```

and

```
Windows might not be able to restart
this operation if it is interrupted.
Check to make sure drive x is not full;
you may need as much as 1.5 MB of free
space to continue.
ID Number: DRVSPACE311
```

the problem is prbably that the files in the hidden FAILSAFE.DRV\FAILSAFE directory on your hard drive are missing and DriveSpace cannot find the MINI.CAB file in your Windows 95 SYSTEM subdirectory. The work-around is to copy the MINI.CAB file from your original Windows 95 distribution media to your **Windows 95** SYSTEM subdirectory.

✔ If you are working in **Windows 95** Explorer, trying to rename, delete, or move a file that has an underscore in its filename, you may get the following error:

```
Error Renaming File
Cannot rename C:\file_: Cannot find the
specified file. Make sure you specify
the correct path and filename.
```

This error occurs when the file name includes extended ANSI characters that Windows Explorer does not recognize. The work-around: open an MS-DOS prompt, and make the changes from the command line using the appropriate ANSI characters.

✔ If **Windows 95** runs correctly for some time, but then it starts displaying a VSERVER 6251 error message, the problem may be a virus, including Forms Virus, Stoned Virus, Generic 21 Virus, and the Monkey Virus. The work-around: you need to run an antivirus program to scan and then clean your system of viruses.

✔ When you run an MS-DOS prompt in a window and press ALT+TAB to switch to another application immediately after pressing the ALT+SPACEBAR key combination (without releasing the ALT key between the two actions), you may find that the title of the application you are switching to remains on the screen in the task-switching window after you release the TAB key. To remove the task-switching window from the screen, you must hit ALT+TAB again.

✔ When you try to load an application, **Windows 95** may report one of the following error messages:

```
Win32 Loader Error
Win32 Exec App unable to find
C:\<directory\filename>
```

where <directory\filename> is the executable file you were trying to start, or

```
Error Starting Program
There is not enough memory to start
(filename). Quit some programs, and then
try again.
```

Additionally, you may receive the following error when you try to close a 32-bit application, such as WordPad:

```
Insufficient memory to perform opera-
tion.
```

These errors occur when the virtual memory settings are too low, according to Microsoft. To correct this problem, increase the virtual memory settings.

¥ Trying to use the extended characters for ANSI code 147 (opening double quotation mark), 148 (closing double quotation mark), or 151 (em-dash) in **Windows 95** generates an incorrect screen character. Use TrueType fonts to display the proper symbols with these characters.

✔ If you receive an error message when you create a file or subdirectory (folder) in the root directory like:

```
Cannot make directory entry - <filename>
```

or

```
<filename>: This filename is not valid.
```

or

```
Unable to create <"New Folder">. Make
sure the disk is not full or read-only.
```

the problem may be that all 512 root directory entries allowed by DOS have been used. Microsoft acknowledges that this problem can also occur with fewer than 512 files and subdirectories in the root because **Windows 95** uses additional directory entries to store long filenames.

✔ The Accessibility utility for **Windows 95** contains several features to assist users who are physically challenged by providing functions such as sticky keys and mouse movement using the keyboard. However, if the accessibility components of Windows 95 are enabled and the system is not compatible with those components, problems can emerge, such as
1) Pressing keys generates system beeps.
2) The ALT and SHIFT keys seem to stick.
3) Using the keypad causes cursor movement and/or opening or closing of applications.
4) An up-siren or down-siren sound is generated.
To disable Windows 95 accessibility components:
1. Click the Start button on the taskbar.
2. Choose Control Panel.
3. Double-click Accessibility Options.
4. Click the check boxes to disable the options one by one.
5. Select the Save Settings box.
6. Click the Apply Now button and OK.

✔ If the DriveSpace compression driver is loaded in memory and the Automatically Mount New Compressed Devices option is enabled, your Compaq computer may take an unusually long time to boot in **Windows 95**. The work-around: either disable the Automatically Mount New Compressed Devices option under Programs / Accessories /System Tools, then DriveSpace. Or change the Power Up

Speed setting on your Compaq computer from Automatic to Full.

✔ When closing MS-DOS-based applications run from an icon in **Windows 95**, the DOS application's window may remain open with the message:

```
Finished - <Application Name>
```

on the title bar of the Window. Microsoft says this is by design, so that you can see any messages, such as errors, that may be generated by the MS-DOS-based application. However, you can change the program properties for the MS-DOS-based application so that it closes on exit. To do this:

1. Use the right (secondary) mouse button to click the icon for the MS-DOS-based application.
2. Choose Properties.
3. Click the Program tab.
4. Click Close On Exit to select that option.
5. Click OK to accept the settings.

✔ If **Windows 95** freezes at the logo screen or Windows 95 reports an error like:

```
Missing HIMEM.SYS
Make sure that the file is in your Windows directory and that its location is correctly specified in your CONFIG.SYS file.
```

the problems is probably that you have the NOAUTO parameter in the DOS= statement in your CONFIG.SYS file. The work-around: change this line from something like:

```
DOS=HIGH,UMB,NOAUTO
```

to something like

```
DOS=HIGH,UMB
```

¥ The UNFORMAT.COM tool from **MS-DOS 5.0** will not work with Windows 95. You must use UNFORMAT.COM from MS-DOS version 6.0 or later.

✔ If you get an error like:

```
Unable to create a shortcut here.
Do you want the shortcut to be placed on
the desktop?
```

When you try to add an application to the **Windows 95** Start menu by performing a drag-and-drop operation to the Start button on the taskbar, the Start Menu folder may be corrupted or has been removed by deleting the C:\WINDOWS\Start Menu directory from MS-DOS. The fix: shut down **Windows 95**. Then click Restart The Computer, and the system will create a new Start Menu folder and re-enable the Start menu. If shutting down and restarting the system does not re-enable the Start menu, Microsoft advises deleting the Start Menu folder and then shutting down and restarting the system again to re-create and re-enable the Start menu.

¥ You can use **Windows 3.x**'s Program Manager with Windows 95, but there are some problems. For instance, when you copy a link or item from the desktop to Program Manager, the item's icon is lost. Also, you cannot drag an item from a Program Manager group to the Windows 95 desktop.

✔ If windows on the screen seem to jump rather than smoothly slide when you reposition them with the mouse in **Windows 95**, run Control Panel, click DeskTop and then check the Granularity (under Sizing Grid). It should be set to 0.

¥ Surprisingly, Microsoft has not made it possible to switch back to the **Windows 95** Explorer Desktop when using Alt-Tab to cycle through all open applications IF you are running two DOS applications full screen (and no Windows apps). So if you have two DOS applications running full screen and are working in one of them; it is only possible to switch back to Explorer by putting the DOS program into a window (Alt-Enter) first. This is one way that Windows 3.1 offered greater ease of use than Windows 95.

¥ Creating a desktop shortcut to a certain folders (generally large ones such as Windows or folders with programs which are not contained in the Registry like DOS applications and **Encarta '94**) and either selecting "Properties" or just using "delete" to try to get rid of the shortcut causes a IPF page fault in Explorer.

¥ The properties set in **Windows 95** Explorer windows (such as view type, auto arrange, window size and location) can spontaneously get lost — they work for a while then ..oops it's back to the dorky "large icon display."

¥ When you upgrade from **Windows for Workgroups**, your shared directories are not maintained and these will need to be reshared in Windows 95.

¥ In the **Windows 95** Desktop Start/Run dialog, dropping the history list down, typing a new string into the edit control and pressing <tab> to change focus, results in loss of the entered string.

✔ Microsoft is apparently under the misapprehension that British Summer Time ends on the fifth Sunday in October. In fact the change should take place on the fourth Sunday (in 1995 on October 22). Because of erroneous English Time Zone data in the registry, many UK users will find their system time changing back to GMT one week later than it should do. The fix is to alter the value of the key StandardStart from "05" to "04" at

```
HLM\System\CurrentControlSet\Control\
TimeZoneInformation (Byte 7)
```

and

```
HLM\Software\Microsoft\Windows\
CurrentVersion\Time Zones\GMT (Byte 19).
```

¥ Microsoft has also used the rather weird name "GMT Daylight Time" instead of the more commonly understood "British Summer Time" in International Settings for the UK. Although this has been fixed in the latest version of Windows NT, the change has not yet made it into Windows 95.

¥ The **Windows 95** Resource Kit incorrectly states that there is no limit to the number of TrueType fonts which can be installed in Windows 95. In fact, John Akers (Microsoft Product Support) has confirmed there is actually a limit of between 1000-1500 fonts (dependent on file size), and installing this many fonts will cause a slowdown in the performance of Windows 95.

✔ When you start a program on a computer that is using disk compression, you may receive an

```
Out of memory
```

error message when running **Windows 95**. To work around this problem, Microsoft advises: "If you are using a Microsoft compression program (DrvSpace or DblSpace), the swap file can be safely placed on the compressed drive (assuming there is enough free space on the compressed drive). If you are using a non-Microsoft compression program, you must enlarge the host drive or move the swap file to another uncompressed drive."

✔ If you only have five icons available (Add New Hardware, System, Modems, ODBC, and Network) when you open Control Panel from a shortcut or another program, the problem is probably that you are running a version of CONTROL.EXE from an earlier version of Windows. The work-around: remove the shortcut that points to the CONTROL.EXE. Then check to see if the CONTROL.EXE file in the Windows folder is the current version (the file should have a 1995 date). If it isn't current, remove or rename it and then extract the current file from the **Windows 95** disks or CD-ROM and place it in the Windows folder.

¥ If you press the ALT+TAB, ALT+ENTER, or ALT+ESC key combination repeatedly while you are running a high-resolution MS-DOS-based graphics program, you may get a garbled or unintelligible display, or the error:

```
This application cannot be restored and
will be terminated.
```

There is no work-around, except to avoid this key combination in **Windows 95**.

✔ According to Microsoft, "When you try to use the CapScrn tool (CAPSCRN.EXE) that is included with **Microsoft Video for Windows version 1.1** and the Video for Windows portion of Microsoft Office Professional version 4.3c, you receive the following error message:

```
Unable to load the capture driver. The
driver is either already in  use, out of
memory, or is not installed."
```

The work-around: edit your SYSTEM.INI to add the following line to the [Drivers] section:

```
MSVIDEO8=SCRNCAP.DRV
```

Then save and close the file and then restart your computer.

✔ If you try to copy a file that has a period as the first character, you will receive the error message:

```
Path not found.
```

The work-around: use **Windows 95** Explorer to copy the file instead of typing a COPY command at an MS-DOS prompt. Or, copy the file using its short filename, and then rename the file.

✔ Sometimes when you close a 16-bit program that is listed as not responding in the **Windows 95**'s Close Program dialog box and then restart the program, you may receive a GPF. The work-around: shut down and entirely turn off your computer system, then restart the computer.

✔ If you select a group of files, use the right mouse button to click the selected group, and choose **Windows 95** Quick View from the menu, some of the files may not be displayed. Instead, you may receive an error message stating that a file is damaged or invalid, or the Quick View window may display a

```
Serious error
```

message. The work-around: view the files individually, rather than as a group of selected files.

¥ If you use the old **Windows 3.1** 16-bit File Manager program (Winfile.exe) to create or modify file associations in Windows 95, certain special file types may not function correctly. Thw work-around: don't use File Manager to create file associations in Windows 95. Instead, use the File Types tab. The Windows 95 interface does not allow the association of special files to be changed.

¥ There is a small cosmetic bug in **Windows 95** which causes the leading zero to be omitted when you are changing the time using the Date/Time tool in Control Panel and you are less than ten minutes after any hour.

✔ If the icons in your Control Panel appear black, or otherwise display incorrectly, the problem may be that your ShellIconCache file in the Windows folder is damaged. To fix the problem:
1. Restart **Windows 95** in Safe mode.
2. Use Windows Explorer to remove the ShellIconCache file from the Windows folder.
3. Restart Windows 95 normally.

✔ You can't access system icons on the **Windows 95** taskbar without using a mouse or some other pointing device. The work-around: use the MouseKeys option to move the mouse pointer, click, double-click, and drag items by means of the numeric keypad. To enable the MouseKeys option:
1. Click the Start button, then click Help.
2. On the Index tab, type
`mousekeys, turning on`
3. Click Display, and then follow the instructions in the Help topic.

✔ If you open the Fonts folder in **Windows 95** Explorer and find the Open, Print, and Install New Font commands are missing from the Fonts folder menus, the problem may be that your FONTEXT.DLL is missing or damaged, causing the menus to contain only the commands for a generic folder. To fix the problem:

1. Restart Windows 95 in MS-DOS mode.
2. Change to the Windows\System folder.
3. If the FONTEXT.DLL file exists, rename it to FONTEXT.OLD.
4. Extract a new copy of the Fontext.dll file from the original Windows 95 disks or CD-ROM to the WINDOWS\SYSTEM folder.

✔ If your icons may seem to change randomly in My Computer or Windows Explorer, or on the desktop, the problem may be caused by an improperly updated icon cache. The work-around: press the F5 key to refresh the icons in the current folder in **Windows 95**.

✔ When you try to delete a folder that is too many levels from the root in **Windows 95**, you may receive the following error message:

```
Cannot remove folder <folder name>:
Access is denied. Make sure the disk is
not full or write protected and that the
file is not currently in use.
```

The work-around: rename some of the parent folders that are closer to the root directory with shorter names, then try to delete the folder.

✔ If you rename a file with a registered extension (for example, a .txt file) in **Windows 95** Explorer or in My Computer, and then you attempt to resize the Windows Explorer or My Computer window, you may receive the following:

```
If you change a filename extension, the
file may become unusable. Are you sure
you want to change it?
```

When you attempt to click either the Yes or No button to clear the Rename dialog box, the dialog box does not clear and the Windows Explorer and/or My Computer window may appear to hang. The work-around: clear the Rename dialog box and return to the Windows Explorer or My Computer window by pressing the Y key (for the Yes button) or the N key (for the No button).

¥ Microsoft acknowledges that "if you create a folder in the Windows\NetHood folder and try to view it using Network Neighborhood, you see another item instead of the folder you are trying to view." There is no work-around in **Windows 95** at present.

✔ If you create a file or folder that contains characters from the extended character set that cannot be converted to ANSI, you may not be able to delete, move, open, or otherwise access that file or folder. Further, when you double-click a folder in **Windows 95** Explorer, you receive the following error message:

```
The file [or folder]<filename>does not
exist.
```

where <filename> is the name of the file in question on your system. The work-around: if you want to delete a file, try to delete the file using the DEL command and "*.*" wildcard designator. Note that this method deletes all the files in the folder containing the file you want to delete, so you should move all the files you want to save to a different folder first.

✔ Each time you start Program Manager in **Windows 95**, you may find that the Program Manager window creeps noticeably higher on the screen, eventually moving itself off the top of screen. According to Microsoft, this problem occurs when the taskbar is positioned at the top of the screen and you have enabled the Always On Top option and disabled the Auto Hide option for the taskbar. The work-around: either move the taskbar to another position on the screen and move the Program Manager window lower on the screen before you close it, or dsable the taskbar's Always On Top option, or enable its Auto Hide option.

✔ If you try to run **Windows 95** Help twice at the same time (e.g., by starting Help from the Start menu, and then opening another Help file from Windows Explorer, you may receive the following error message:

```
Winhelp: This program has performed an
illegal operation and will be shut down.
If the problem persists, contact the
program vendor.
```

The work-around: don't try to run two instances of Help at the same time.

✔ If you get the following error message when you try to start **Windows 95**:

```
Insufficient memory to initialize Win-
dows. Quit one or more memory-resident
programs or remove unnecessary utilities
from your CONFIG.SYS and AUTOEXEC.BAT
files, and restart your computer.
```

the problem is probably a low-memory situation caused by real-mode drivers loaded in memory, or the hard disk containing the swap file is low on free space. The work-around: remove unnecessary drivers from the

AUTOEXEC.BAT and CONFIG.SYS files, restart your computer, and then try to start Windows 95 again.

✔ When you run a text-mode mouse program like the Multi-Edit editor as a full-screen program in **Windows 95**, the mouse pointer may slowly move toward the upper left-hand corner of the screen. The work-around: press ALT+ENTER to run the program in a window.

¥ If you use the XCOPY command to copy a file to or from a floppy disk, you may receive the following error message:

```
Invalid path
```

even if the Path is correct. This error may also occur if your floppy disk drive does not contain a disk, your floppy disk drive door is open, your floppy disk is not properly formatted, or your floppy disk is damaged.

✔ If when you try to start **Windows 95**, you receive the following error message:

```
You cannot run this version of Windows
on DOS 6.x or earlier.
```

the problem is probably that WIN.COM has been added to the Setver table with a version parameter less than 7.00. The work-around:

1. Start Windows 95 in MS-DOS mode.
2. Type the following command, and then press ENTER:
setver win.com /d
3. Restart your computer normally.

✔ If you receive an error like:

```
There is not enough memory to load the
registry.
```

when you start **Windows 95**, the problem may be a corrupt system registry on your computer. The work-around:

1. Restart the computer. When you see the "Starting Windows 95" message, press the F8 key, then choose "Safe mode command prompt only" from the Startup menu.
2. If Windows 95 is installed in the WINDOWS directory on drive C, type the following line, followed by the ENTER key:
```
regedit /l:c:\windows\system.dat /e
c:\system.txt
```
3. If Windows 95 is installed in the WINDOWS directory on drive C and you want to import the SYSTEM.TXT file from the root directory of drive C, type:
regedit /l:c:\windows\system.dat c:\system.txt
4. Restart Windows 95 normally.

¥ If you run DOSSHELL in a **Windows 95** MS-DOS box, you will receive the following error message when you try to start a program from DOSSHELL:
```
Bad Command or Filename
```
because the version of COMMAND.COM included with Windows 95 is incompatible with DOSSHELL. There is no work-around at present.

✔ If you receive an error like:
```
Folder <Folder Name> does not exist.
```
when you try to access a folder on a remote **Windows 95** computer, the problem is probably that the name of the remote folder is identical to the volume label of the remote drive that contains the folder. The work-around: either change the volume label of the remote drive, or rename the remote folder.

✔ After you select a screen saver and click the **Windows 95** Preview button, if you immediately move the mouse, the screen saver Preview button may not function, or the screen saver sample is not animated. The work-around: close the Display Properties dialog box by clicking the OK or the Cancel button, and then open the Display Properties dialog box again.

✔ After working in MS-DOS mode, you may receive an error like:

```
Not ready reading drive <x>. Abort,
Retry, Fail?
```

(where <x> is the floppy drive letter) or

```
Error:MSGSRV32 has performed an illegal
operation.
```

or your system may freeze when you return to the graphical interface of **Windows 95**. This only happens when the active drive is an empty floppy disk drive when you quit MS-DOS mode. The work-around: make sure there is a disk in the floppy drive.

¥ There is a bug in Windows 95's OLE 2.0 object linking and embedding technology that can cause chunks of data from previously deleted files to show up in new files created by some Windows 95 applications, including **Microsoft Office 95**. According to a story by Stephen Manes in the New York Times, the stray chunks of data that can appear come from previously deleted files. The stray information can't be seen in Word 95 or other Office applications, but it can be seen when viewing the raw data in Office files with other applications, such as the Microsoft NotePad text editor. Microsoft plans to issue a fix soon.

✔ The XCOPY32 command does not prompt the user before overwriting files, as all previous version of the DOS COPY command have done. The work-around: use the

`/-Y`

switch with the XCOPY32 command, or use Windows Explorer to copy files, or go back to the old XCOPY command.

¥ **Windows 95** Briefcase does not copy correctly to user profiles if these are set up after Briefcase has been installed. The work around is to delete the original Briefcase icon from the desktop and create a new one by right-clicking on the Desktop and selecting New / Briefcase.

✔ If you use DriveSpace to compress a hard disk containing files which have been added to the **Windows 95** Briefcase, the link between the files and the Briefcase will be broken. The files still exist but will need reassociating with the Briefcase.

✔ If you find that Scan Disk (or indeed System Defragmenter) restarts continually without making progress, it may be that you have a background process running (such as a screen saver, mail, or fax program) which is periodically writing to the hard-disk. The only work-rounds are to temporarily quit these programs or schedule the disk utilities for a time when they are not running.

✔ ScanDisk for **Windows 95** will freeze and display the error

```
Check was stopped because of an error
(255)
```

if it is pre-configured to check a disk drive which no longer exists (e.g. if it is removed by undocking a laptop or uncompressing a Drivespace drive). The work-around: deselect the missing drive and click an alternate one to check.

✔ ScanDisk for **Windows 95** may report errors about files or the folders they reside in, if these have been created or named while using different code pages (e.g., if they have been created with a code page of ASCII character set from another part of the world). If this occurs Microsoft recommends deselecting the "Check Files For Invalid File Names" option in the Advanced dialog box. Normally this should be selected or else the ability of ScanDisk to detect or repair seriously damaged folders will be inhibited.

¥ ScanDisk conflicts with the TSR installed by **AT&T Mail 2.5** or earlier, preventing it from repairing disk problems. Microsoft suggests contacting AT&T for information about an upgraded version.

✔ If a backup to tape proceeds at less than 1.5 MB per minute in **Windows 95**, the tape streamer may be conflicting with the computer video card. Microsoft suggests a work-around is to start the backup and then open an MS-DOS box full-screen, keeping it in the foreground until the operation has finished.

✔ **Windows 95** Help, Windows Explorer, and the Disk Tools all have links to the Windows 95 Backup program. If this is not installed, but the MS-DOS BACKUP.EXE program is present on the System Path, these links will automatically start the MS-DOS Backup program. This problem can be avoided by moving the DOS backup program into a folder which is not on the Path.

¥ If a computer is set up with different profiles to support multiple users, be aware that although some elements of Desktop Themes, such as background wallpaper or screen colors, are saved on a per-user basis, desktop icons and screen savers from the Theme are not, so all users of this computer will have to use these items.

✔ Many users are creating ASCII file backups of the registry using the command:

```
REGEDIT /E <filename>
```

hoping this will give protection in case they need to restore it later using

```
REGEDIT /C <filename>
```

However extensive tests suggest this method is not totally reliable. Problems experienced when rebuilding the registry this way include: machine lockups when reimporting the ASCII file; memory allocation errors in DOS followed by the system rebooting; error messages such as:

```
not enough memory to load the registry
the registry is corrupt
```

when restarting **Windows 95** with a rebuilt database; and mystery loss of program features such as the Quickview option from an Explorer file right-click menu, and Excel 95's ability to parse a long filename when autoloading.

✔ As another example of mysterious, untraceable occurrences presumably caused by small corruptions of the registry database: the option to QuickView files on the **Windows 95** Explorer right-click menu of all viewable files, which may |suddenly vanish for no obvious reason. According to the Windows Setup Tab, however, QuickView may still indicate it is installed. This QuickView menu item can be restored by removing and reinstalling the component.

Index

Symbols

A

B

C

D

E

F

G

H

L

M

N

O

P

Q

R

S

T

U

V

W

X

Don't Face Them Alone.

Get BugNet

It's a buggy world out there. Protect yourself with BugNet, the global resource for PC bugs, glitches, incompatibilities... and their fixes.

Only BugNet gives you fixes for thousands of bugs in popular off-the-shelf software. Ask us about our monthly newsletter (in both print and electronic form), our BugNet BugMaster Database, and the searchable electronic version of The Windows 95 Bug Collection.

"It's is a must-have subscription." – John Dvorak

P.O. Box 393 Sumas, WA 98295
bugnet@bugnet.com
http://www.bugnet.com/~bugnet